Yacht Clubs of the World

Yacht Clubs of the World

On the Water — In the Clubhouse — The World Over

PETER JOHNSON

First published in Great Britain 1994
by Waterline Books
an imprint of Airlife Publishing Ltd.,
101 Longden Road, Shrewsbury, England

ISBN 1 85310 333 0

A Sheerstrake Production

A CIP catalogue record of this book
is available from the British Library

Printed in Singapore by Kyodo Printing Co. (S'pore) Pte. Ltd.

also by Peter Johnson

Passage Racing
Ocean Racing and Offshore Yachts
Yachtsman's Guide to the Rating Rule
Boating Britain
The Guinness Book of Yachting Facts and Feats
The Guinness Guide to Sailing
Yachting World Handbook
Offshore Manual International
This is Fast Cruising
The Encyclopedia of Yachting
Whitbread Round the World 1973-1993

The author is a member of the:
Cruising Association, Junior Offshore Group, Royal Lymington Yacht Club,
Royal Ocean Racing Club, Royal Yacht Squadron.

The author was elected to these clubs, served as a member and, in due
course, resigned:
Dhekelia Yacht Club, Carlton Club, Inter-Services YC, Island SC, Lymington
Town Sailing Club, Royal Air Force YC, Royal Artillery YC, Royal Southern YC.

Acknowledgments

It was simply not possible to visit every club described in this work and I am immensely grateful to all those club officers, secretaries or chief executives who so kindly sent me material on their respective yacht and sailing clubs. What was sent was fascinating and I only regret that I am unable to use every word of it. To those important clubs which did not reply to me, I can only say I fully understand; running a club is in its own way twice as hard as running a business. There are no holidays in the sailing season! Where I visited clubs in several countries, I thank those I met for their time and enthusiasm. The quote from the novel *Dead Reckoning* by Sam Llewellyn is by kind permission of the publisher, Michael Joseph Ltd. Brigadier Miles Hunt-Davis CBE, of the staff of HRH Prince Philip at Buckingham Palace, kindly supplied the number of clubs in which His Royal Highness is concerned worldwide.

Illustrations

Black and white line drawings by Ray Harvey BSc, CEng, MRINA.

Photographs by photographer and page number: Mike Balmforth 24, 27; Beken of Cowes 33, 76; Tony Blachford 95; Hugh Bourn 35; Christel Clear 22, 54 (top) 102 (bottom), 116 (bottom), 144 (top), 151; Barry Duffield 137 (both); Jonathan Eastland 73, 87; John Evans 60 (bottom); Christian Février 40; Guy Gurney 54 (bottom), 57, 68, 92; Peter Johnson 10, 38, 46, 48 (bottom), 52, 74 (top), 108, 123 (top), 129, 133, 135, 139 (top), 157, 160; Theo Kampa 29, 78; Kos 70, 96, 153; Roger Lean-Vercoe 20, 129; New Zealand Govt. 155; W. M. Nixon 74 (bottom), 139 (bottom), 142; Thomas-Oxford 126; Rick Tomlinson 60 (top), 64, 113 (top), 115; Whitbread plc 144 (bottom); Respective clubs 24, 31, 42, 44, 48 (top), 80, 89 (both), 102, 106, 111, 119, 121, 146 (both), 149.

"1st June 1815 at the Thatched House Tavern, St James's, London, the following resolutions were entered into:

First, that the club be called the Yacht Club."

-original minute of the Royal Yacht Squadron, 1815.

"He parked by the yacht club door and went in... Then I saw the club secretary, looking grim and shaking his head. His voice floated down the quay. 'Out', he was saying. 'Or I'll call the police.'

'Hmm', said Breen. 'My friends thought something like this might happen. Barred by the committee.'

I sat down on a bollard. Sally looked at me, the dark hair swinging on either side of her cheekbones, her eyes full of secret amusement. I knew that what she was thinking was the same as what I was thinking. We did not give a monkey's for yacht clubs. Pulteney was home and that was that.

'Would you like a drink at the club?' said Breen.

'No thank you', I said. 'Let's go to the *Mermaid*. The beer's better'."

- from the novel *Dead Reckoning* by Sam Llewellyn, 1987.

Contents

Welcome to the club

Yacht club!

Depending on your view point, the words conjure up exclusiveness and snobbery, fun in small boats, the bray of the cocktail party and throb of the dance band, a welcome hot meal after a soaking in salt water, where youngsters learn to sail, strange and complex rules afloat and ashore, foreign visitors, flags, rescue boats.

For sailors and also for socialites, it can admit to all these things, but a lot more and many less passing characteristics. Clubs of any kind are where one meets friends and even if not every member is known, one can sit at the same table or strike up a conversation, in a way not usual in a pub or restaurant, for you are equals elected on the same basis. For yacht clubs this means an enthusiasm for the sea, lake or river and sailing or boating upon it.

This book tells of the entertaining variety of many yacht and sailing clubs in different parts of the world. Each is fashioned to the needs of its members; almost every one has a tradition and a history which is remarkable. The words 'yacht club' do not necessarily appear in the title, which may use the 'sailing club', 'association', 'group', 'racing club', or in the case of non-English speaking countries 'Société des Régates', 'Sejl Klub..' or equivalent. Yet the English wording often prevails, the most senior and one of the original clubs of France being simply 'Yacht Club de France' and in Buenos Aires we have 'Yacht Club Argentino'. The term did not exist (see 'oldest club' in next section) until some English aristocrats and gentlemen met in 1815 and resolved to form a club. There existed a number of clubs such as Boodle's, Buck's and Brook's and they hit on a name for theirs; it was the Yacht Club. Others followed, the first being the Thames Yacht Club in 1823.

A definition of a yacht club (from now on the term includes sailing, boating etc clubs) is today one recognized by its national authority. There is a technical reason for this, since to use the rules of yacht racing one needs to be bound to them via his or her membership of a club, of its attachment to the national authority and thence to the international authority, the International Yacht Racing Union (IYRU). Thus the rule structure, is in theory held together. In this book we survey only clubs, however they may be named: not national authorities, not class (classes of yacht) associations.

In the earliest days, one reason for forming clubs was to insure agreed rules between yachts competing, their owners being like-minded people, who were no longer in the hands of the old professional skippers and crews. Today the racing and rating rules have become national or international; most races are 'open' (though by no means all) and the old problems of professionals and people with ideas different from those of the organizers has returned in modern form. The professionals themselves, constricted as they see it, by the yacht club, sometimes break away and form 'shell' clubs of their own. This has happened in the *America*'s Cup where a New Zealand syndicate sailed under the flag of the Mercury Bay Boating Club, whose clubhouse was a rusty Ford car on a beach. A British leading owner retains for his use at any time (and used it for a 1993 Admiral's Cup challenge), the Crusader Yacht Club, which has no known location!

Though rules vary, if you are a member of one club, you are usually admitted to any other, almost certainly if you arrive by sea, probably if you are from abroad, less certainly if you are passing on dry land. The extent of welcome for a sailor is usually considerable from members, but may be constricted by the rules of the club and the laws of the state or country. A number of clubs have 'reciprocal' arrangements with others, which appears to mean that members can use each other's premises freely. The Royal Hong Kong Yacht Club probably has the biggest list of any, maybe because of its geographical position. It has reciprocals in Asia, Australia, Britain, Europe and the USA! Since a visitor to any club has to seek permission, even if it is a simple signing of a book, it is hard to see what reciprocity does, except express good will. Some clubs, especially those in London and New York for obvious reasons, will have nothing of it. On regatta days or over a series, clubs will usually declare the all competitors are honorary members of the club for the period.

Any club is by definition exclusive. That is why it receives special privileges from the law, harbour authorities and others. There are those with very limited membership, say a few hundred, where it is 'difficult' to get in (Larchmont Yacht Club) and there are those quite actively recruiting (Cruising Association); I saw a wide banner across the building of one Florida sailing club announcing a membership drive week!

Many clubs have a rule banning any business in the club, but this can hardly be realistic. The border between social and business talk is a blurred one and obviously yacht owners are going sometimes to discuss topics other than their favourite anti-fouling or how to deal with non-sailing wives. Some American clubs recognize the difficulty and merely say that business papers must not be displayed; some Australian clubs go further and make some rooms available for business discussions. It is a matter of the culture of the country and traditions of the club.

Most yacht clubs are mainly male. By that is meant that women in many clubs have equal status, but in practice are seldom flag officers and are almost always a small minority on committees. In the early days clubs were exclusively for men; women hardly allowed on the premises. Some such as the Royal Bermuda Yacht Club continue in this way. Ladies cannot use certain parts of the Royal Thames Yacht Club including the main front staircase. In Australia the leading clubs only allow ladies as 'associate members' and in general their activities are separate from those of the sailors and include such items as fashion shows and harbour trips by steamer. Around the world, the paid executive secretary on the other hand can frequently be a woman.

Many clubs have produced, usually on some anniversary, their own history. The New York Yacht Club, Seawanhaka Corinthian Yacht Club and others have heavy hard bound volumes. Other clubs have a simple leaflet. All though are of immense value, especially to new members, responsible officers of the club and others who will surely be influenced by those who came before them.

This book has picked out a limited number of yacht clubs whose doings are of significance and whose story is entertaining. Another equal number might have been chosen, but the author presents the selected clubs as a survey that has never before been attempted. There are indeed thousands more, many serving local, company or particular sailing needs. The British national authority (Royal Yachting Association) lists (1993) about 1,240 recognized clubs and associations (some 148 being class associations). The American national authority (US Sailing Association, formerly US Yacht Racing Union) lists 1,980 including 170 class associations. These tremendous numbers are no doubt equal to the rest of the world put together, but countries such as Australia, France, Germany each have several hundred recognized clubs.

The courses they steer

Club officers

In the English speaking world the president of a yacht club is the commodore and then there are one or more vice commodores and rear commodores. A few do not abide by this convention and have a president (Cruising Association) or even Captain (Junior Offshore Group). Abroad terms vary, but in France it is always president. These officers have special flags and again the English speakers follow naval parlance and refer to flag officers. Flag usage varies with special flags in America, but in Britain the club burgee in swallow tail form for the commodore and balls inserted for the vice and rear commodores. Many clubs have a higher position used for some member of eminence or long service to the club known as Admiral, though again usage varies. His flag is a rectangular version of the club burgee. A club has secretary, chief executive, general manager or other term for the permanent executive in its office. In the USA the commodore tends to have a one year appointment, in Britain three or four; on the continent, once in, he seems to stay for many years.

Royal patronage

In countries with monarchies, especially in western Europe, there is a long tradition of association with yachting and yacht racing. Members of several royal families are seen every year sailing in major events. Queen Elizabeth II who does not sail is Patron of several clubs. The Dutch, Danish, Norwegian, Spanish and Swedish sovereigns have honorary titles in clubs of their nations. The King of Greece (exiled) sails in England, where he lives, and elsewhere. The Princess Royal, an active sailor and boat owner is the only female honorary member of the Royal Yacht Squadron and admiral and patron of several clubs and president of the Royal Yachting Association. The Prince of Wales is Commodore of the Royal Thames Yacht Club; but it is Prince Philip, Admiral and previously commodore of the Royal Yacht Squadron, who races at Cowes every year, who over the years has been in demand as admiral, president or honorary member of many clubs in Britain and other parts of the world. He has such a position in no less than fifty-eight of them.

Some clubs are royal and others equally distinguished are not. In a number of countries such as Belgium, Holland, the Scandinavian nations and Spain, as well as countries outside Europe such as Brunei and Thailand, the 'royal' title is apparently given to just a few leading clubs. In Britain, Canada, Australia, New Zealand and elsewhere in the Commonwealth, there are however a large number of 'royal' clubs. The fact is that most of these were granted the title in the 19th century and have kept it ever since. After the reign of Queen Victoria, the British and Commonwealth government departments responsible (a recommendation goes through plenty of officials before the sovereign is asked to approve) have been far more sparing. The Royal Lymington Yacht Club and Royal Ocean Racing Club were both founded only in 1925; they are among the few 20th century created 'royal' clubs. Some of the early clubs had been visited by Queen Victoria or Prince Albert, or given their patronage. Later there were clubs which had given races for the royal racing cutter *Britannia*. In the then colonies, senior clubs were well regarded by the colonial office, which made the recommendation. A special British ensign (see 'Flags') can be carried by any club so allowed and is not directly connected with being royal. Most 'royal' clubs do have such an ensign.

A club can carry the royal title without having any member of the royal family in any position. By contrast, in Monaco, the royal family are patrons and flag officers, but the club is not 'royal'. In Japan, there is no royal tradition in yachting, despite the ancient monarchy.

Dress

This is a jungle and varies widely between clubs and countries. It does however often play a part in clubs, perhaps harking back to the naval tradition. Some lay down strict laws; some require jacket and tie (any jacket, any tie) after, say, 1800 every evening. Some have uniforms. For instance the Royal Canadian Yacht Club has elaborate dress rules with rooms of the club which require formal attire. Its 'summer dress' is blue reefer, plain white shirt, black tie, cream trousers, white belt, white or cream socks. When a cap is mentioned it is 'of similar pattern as worn by the Royal Yacht Squadron'. There is dress laid down for juniors.

At the Royal Perth Yacht Club, Western Australia, all crews on yachts have to wear whites. The flag officers have rank badges rather like the navy which they display in summer (shoulder boards) and winter uniforms. In Scandinavia and many American clubs, flag officers have rank badges in black braid on their sleeves, visible but not conspicuous. In Britain flag officers have no badges and all forms of badge on a blazer pocket are 'bad form'; many clubs give the flag officers a gold and enamel tie pin in the form of his flag officer's flag to wear and that shows his rank. Black buttons with the club crest (which you can then never see!) are correct in Britain and elsewhere (brass buttons are for paid hands!). It is believed that King Edward VII started this custom. France and Latin countries seldom go in for this pseudo-naval attire.

Flags

Every yacht club in the world has a burgee; that is a triangular flag to its own pattern. This is flown from the top of a flag mast at the club with the national ensign on a yard arm. This is even done in cities, certainly at waterside premises. Members fly the burgee on their boats in accordance with club and national custom. The customary position is on a spreader, but a few clubs insist the burgee must be at the masthead; this is often difficult with modern electronic and wind indicating equipment.

Some countries have a yacht ensign, for instance the USA. This signifies that the vessel is a pleasure yacht and is non-commercial and should be accorded privileges (e.g. no commercial harbour dues). The Netherlands has several ensigns depending on the club, usually the national tricolour defaced by some badge. The United Kingdom and Commonwealth have a confusing mass of national ensigns, many yacht clubs having

their own pattern. There is no logic in these. Admittedly what might be termed 'leading clubs' usually have them, but then other distinguished clubs do not. It is not necessary to be royal to have what is called 'an Admiralty warrant'; that is a special ensign.

The ordinary British ensign is a red ensign. A special ensign may be this red one with a club badge in it, which is called 'defaced'. Some clubs have a defaced blue ensign. A few clubs have the undefaced blue ensign. Members of the Royal Yacht Squadron only can fly a white ensign. Note that a number of British institutions (Customs, Port authorities etc) also have defaced ensigns. For a brief history of how the yacht club ensigns came about see page 63, Royal Yacht Squadron.

There is a view that these many yacht ensigns serve little purpose today. Only the members of the club concerned seem to know what they mean. If they were suspended and a single British yacht ensign, which, unlike the others, would become widely known, was designed, it would be a sensible change.

Names

The most obvious names are those simply after the locality of the club: Hamble River Sailing Club, Royal Lymington Yacht Club, Fremantle Sailing Club, Key Biscayne Yacht Club, Port Huron Yacht Club, Société des Régates Rochelaises. There are thousands of them. Other refer to a more general area or even a nation: Royal Northern Yacht Club, Royal Southern Yacht Club, Eastern Yacht Club, Royal Dorset Yacht Club, Royal Danish Yacht Club, Royal Swedish Yacht Club. Then there was a period in Victorian times when some clubs were named after members of the royal family: Royal Alfred Yacht Club (Australia), Royal Victoria Yacht Club (Isle of Wight). The Queen Mary Sailing Club is named after the already-named Queen Mary reservoir on which it is sited. Or non-royals: Ida Lewis Yacht Club.

There are regimental and service clubs: Royal Armoured Corps Yacht Club, United States Navy Sailing Association, Royal Air Force Sailing Association, Royal Air Force Yacht Club. Companies, schools and other organizations: Bar Yacht Club (lawyers), Charterhouse Sailing Club (school), Barclays Bank Sailing Club, University of Minnesota Yacht Club.

There are the clubs named after what they do, but which are 'national': Cruising Club of America, Royal Cruising Club, Royal Ocean Racing Club, Nippon Ocean Racing Club, Wooden Boat Racing Association, Windward Sailing Club (?!).

Around the world are those clubs which use instead the word 'squadron': Royal Nova Scotia Yacht Squadron, Royal New Zealand Yacht Squadron, Royal Sydney Yacht Squadron, Awosting Yacht Squadron (New Jersey), Royal Minquiers Yacht Squadron (St Malo, France), Westhampton Yacht Squadron (NY), Royal Yacht Squadron.

For all the words used, a glance at complete lists of clubs in the English speaking world shows that 'yacht club' is still by far the most popular over 'sailing club' or any kind of 'association'. Although the term 'yacht club' is sometimes felt to be elitist or discouraging to would-be sailors, at the end of the day it but a technical term most widely used for the kind of organization surveyed here.

Corinthian

This term is in the title of several clubs. It essentially means 'amateur' in the best sense of the word. In May 1872 the Corinthian Yacht Club was founded in London for sailing on the wider reaches of the London River and within a year had 200 members, with a clubhouse based at Erith. It became the Royal Corinthian Yacht Club in 1892 and is now in a large building at Burnham-on-Crouch. There is a London Corinthian Sailing Club very active on the Thames in west London, described on page 37. The Seawanhaka Corinthian Yacht Club at Oyster Bay, NY, proud of its amateur status and expertise, was founded in 1871 as the Seawanhaka Yacht Club (page 91) and added the word Corinthian in 1882. The name had been rejected by the members in 1874, but strangely the regattas were called 'Corinthian Races' i.e. non-professional. Around the English-speaking world a few clubs pop up with the word in their title: Mushroom Corinthian Yacht Club, Clyde Corinthian Yacht Club, Dundee Corinthian Boating Club (all Scotland), Cowes Corinthian Yacht Club, Royal Plymouth Corinthian Yacht Club, Unqua Corinthian Yacht Club (NY), Wolfeboro Corinthian Yacht Club (Maine), Corinthian Yacht Club of Seattle, Corinthian Yacht Club of St Francisco, Pacific Corinthian Yacht Club (South California).

In *Yacht and Boat Sailing* by Dixon Kemp, published in 1878, the author defined 'Corinthian' as 'a term in yacht parlance synonymous with amateur. The term Corinthian half a century ago was commonly applied to the aristocratic patrons of sports, some of which such as pugilism, are not now the fashion. The name was adopted in consequence of the similarity between the fashionable young men of Corinth who emulated the feats of athletes and their modern prototypes. Some clubs in Corinthian matches do not allow any paid hands to be on board.'

Oldest club

The earliest club still in existence is generally agreed to be the Royal Cork Yacht Club (page 58). This is true if one accepts that it is the same society as the Cork Harbour Water Club, whose foundation date is unknown, but which was functioning in 1720. Its activities were not continuous and it was re-formed in 1828 as the Cork Yacht Club, quickly being given the royal prefix.

In July 1772 Viscount Courtenay, Sir Lawrence Park and twenty-seven local notables founded the Starcross Club (not 'yacht'), which could have been a kind of dinner club, as indeed was the Cork Harbour Water Club by some of its descriptions. They probably held local rowing and sailing contests though the first on record was the Fête Marine of 11th August 1775 (see Appendix I). It is stated in the *Exeter Flying Post* newspaper of the time that his lordship's 'yacht' was present. At some stage in the early 19th century the club split from the dining club or became anyway the Starcross Yacht Club, (the only evidence being a trophy cup with the name dated 1832) which has existed ever since.

In 1749, the Prince of Wales (later George III) gave a cup for twelve yachts to have a race on the Thames. Records fade until 1775, when the Duke of Cumberland, his brother, gave a silver cup for a race which involved twenty boats of from two to five tons on the river. He gave such a cup every year until 1782 and a club became formed, known as the Cumberland Sailing Society. The races continued and the members devised a suitable uniform and a commodore was appointed; the main task of the latter was to lead the fleet after the race to a suitable mooring point (usually Vauxhall Gardens), hence the use of the term in English yachting. By 1823 the society had changed its name to the Coronation Society in honour of the coronation of King George IV. That year there was a serious dispute over a race which resulted in a split, a number of members forming a new club called the Thames Yacht Club. The Coronation Society faded away by 1827, while the Thames Yacht Club became royal by order of the new King William IV in 1830 and is the Royal Thames Yacht Club of today.

The history of the formation of the Royal Yacht Squadron is told on page 63. The fact is that it was formed in 1815, never looked back and had none of the breaks of the above clubs. It was called the Yacht Club, a totally new term. This was subsequently copied by others, such as the Thames. What is now the Squadron became the Royal Yacht Club in 1820, the first ever royal yacht club and still the first 'yacht club' and the Royal Yacht Squadron by order of William IV in 1833.

Which then is the oldest yacht club in the world? Is it the Water Club with its breaks and revival? Is it Starcross, a club since 1772? Is it the Royal Thames, if it is the true inheritor of the Cumberland fleet? Or is it the Royal Yacht Squadron, created by the aristocrats of the then leading power in the world and who first and shrewdly put together the words 'yacht' and 'club', thus exactly describing their intentions and who have been thus followed ever since.

Largest number of members

Very many clubs have a membership between 800 and about 1,800. Such a figure seems manageable and results from the 'yachting density' in the area near the club. No doubt there is some club unknown to the author with a record membership, but it appears that the largest number is that of the Royal Hong Kong Yacht Club at 7,956, followed by the Royal Naval Sailing Association with 7,300. The Nippon Ocean Racing Club and the Cruising Association (London) each have 5,000. For small clubs one might pick those that limit their membership as policy, such as the Seawanhaka Corinthian Yacht Club and Royal Yacht Squadron at 450 each; then in this book is the Imperial Poona Yacht Club with twenty-six members in Britain and ninety-seven elsewhere. Maybe the Crusader Yacht Club (previous) has about three yacht crews: quite big yachts, so maybe three dozen?

If any reader knows what might be the biggest or smallest membership of a yacht club in the world, the author would like to hear.

Note on entries

After the introduction on the club, each one is described as follows:

Clubhouse: A description of the present clubhouse. Some clubs have more than one, for instance a town house and also a sailing base. Some clubs have no clubhouse.

Waterside: The immediate marina, dinghy park and anchorage, but sometimes the nearby sailing waters, where these are responsible for the club's situation.

History: Some clubs have volumes of this! So here is a selective summary including previous clubhouses, the founding and early days, previous names, if any. Historic classes and regattas are mentioned and the influence of the club on wider yachting. Sometimes there is talk of personalties, though this is an invidious business. Many fine people have contributed to their own club and I apologise that they are not mentioned. Also there is simply not space to describe famous races and their outcome, which can be found in other books and old magazines. This has to be essentially the story of the yacht club itself.

Classes: The regular yacht and dinghy racing classes of the club, sailed every season. There are border line cases where a club gives races for classes from elsewhere on its regatta days only.

Events and regattas: The doings of the club in the current seasons. Activities vary and the author regrets if particular races or happenings have been omitted. The information is based usually on that supplied by the club, often in its fixture list. Again some selectivity has been necessary.

Members: The approximate number stated for 1992 or 1993. Any special categories of member. If the senior 'ranks' are not the conventionally called commodore etc, then what they are known as. Royal or other patrons, admirals. Other persons' names are not given, as they are for ever changing.

Address: The address of the clubhouse, or the secretary, if he or she operates from elsewhere. The person's name is not given, because of inevitable changes.

Where lengths of boats and other objects are given these are in feet with metric equivalent in brackets. Miles always refer to nautical miles, unless otherwise stated. The length of a boat is its LOA (length overall), unless otherwise stated such as LWL (length on load waterline). The opportunity is taken to refer to nearby or other clubs in the texts, where they are not tabulated in full. Abbreviations are kept to a minimum but the author has used YC for yacht club; SC for sailing club and obvious club abbreviations, but only where the full name has been mentioned in the same text. Cruiser-racers and offshore racers are stated as using the following rating rules: CHS, Channel Handicap System (an Anglo-French rule); IMS, International Measurement System (authorized by the International Offshore Racing Council, London); IOR, International Offshore Rule (same body); PHRF, Performance Handicap Racing Fleet (a rule in wide use in the USA and also, though with different numbers, in New Zealand). Classes with the prefix 'International' are recognized by the IYRU (International Yacht Racing Union, London).

The order of the clubs which have been surveyed is as if we were visiting them over the years, racing and cruising. It is not for me to determine any order of merit, seniority, influence or interest. If it was alphabetical, well that is a job for indexers; by country, it would be too predictable; by age, but we are not studying fossils.

At the end of the book are indexes of clubs, classes and subjects. There are also some appendices of a few historic documents from yacht clubs.

Royal Western Yacht Club of England

One of the world's oldest yacht clubs and amongst those which remain conspicuous with an active membership and as an organizer of international events. The club has always been the principal one in the superb natural harbour of Plymouth.

As the harbour has always been able to accommodate any number of yachts, is sited geographically 150 miles from the open Atlantic and provides safe access in all weather, the club has taken a leading part in the starts or finishes of great ocean races, notably the Fastnet from 1925 and its own short-handed races from 1960. The words 'of England' are needed, as there is a Royal Western in Scotland. In the last century, there was an Irish branch of the 'Western' on the River Shannon.

Clubhouse

This was opened in 1990 and is the first floor of a modern building with offices, chandleries and brokers in Queen Anne's Battery marina. It is purpose built with a large dining room overlooking Plymouth Sound. The previous clubhouse, opened by HRH Prince Philip in 1965, overlooked the Sound, but had no berthing. (It was once the 'public baths'.) Forty-nine years earlier, a clubhouse was opened in a Victorian building up on the Hoe, a raised cliff dominating the harbour. It was damaged in successive air raids and finally destroyed by incendiary bombs along with much of Plymouth on 22nd April 1941. The first place the club had met in the 1830s was a room in the 'Exchange', then at the Royal Hotel - *'which being found not only inconvenient to members but derogatory to its respectability'*, it moved to a house at *'Millbay, which commanded a beautiful view of the sea and breakwater'*.

Waterside

With the clubhouse inside a marina, with numerous berths for large yachts and ample hardstanding, berthing not far from the club is usually possible. Sometimes the marina makes room for big fleets waiting to start, or which have just finished races. When leaving the marina, a yacht is still in protected water and indeed remains so while she can sail around, hoist sail, and so on in Plymouth Sound.

Access from land is slightly out of the way, in the sense that it is a little way from the shops, restaurants and harbour front. There is at times a small ferry from the marina across to the Barbican, an attractive area of narrow streets, pubs and restaurants, as well as the fishing harbour.

History

The origins of the club lie in 'The Port of Plymouth Royal Clarence Regatta Club' formed in 1827. By 1842, the present name was in use and the club had the burgee and ensign used to this day. The ensign is the British Blue Ensign, without any badge or 'defacement', which is not common for clubs and considered a mark of privilege. The club race course, as was often the custom in those days was fixed regardless of wind direction to be *'from a vessel moored off the Hoe, leaving Drake's Island to starboard to Penlee Point and the Drag Stone, thence to the Shag Stone and to the starting vessel; twice or thrice*

Major races often gather before the start or after the finish in the marina at the Royal Western Yacht Club.

round, the length being about thirteen miles, the whole of which may be seen from the Hoe'.

In 1900 there were 382 members including twelve Admirals, fourteen Generals, two Earls, four other Peers and six Baronets. Club regattas were confined to one day in August; in that year three boats owned by members took part. However the Royal Marines band played on the club lawn. In 1903, a proposal to install electric lighting in the club was turned down by a general meeting.

In 1925, the first Fastnet Race finished at the clubhouse and the new Ocean Racing Club was formed by the competitors after the race. In 1934, the J-class, including *Britannia*, owned by King George V, raced in a club regatta for the last time. (Class J, which originated in the USA, only raced between 1930 and 1937, being in effect an *America*'s Cup class).

In the early fifties, the popularity of passage and ocean racing gave a new life to the club with races along the coast and across to France. In 1960 the first single-handed transatlantic race was started by the club. In 1961 it amalgamated with the Royal South Western Yacht Club. Sir Francis Chichester started and finished on the club line, his pioneering single-handed voyage round the world with only one stop. In 1966, the club started its first two-handed round Britain race. HRH The Princess Royal opened the new clubhouse on 24th May 1989.

Classes
Sigma 33, Impala, J24, local handicap.

Events and regattas
Dinghy and small class national and international championships in the Sound. Offshore and passage races along coasts to the east and west and to Brittany. A regular race to Santander, Spain. The biennial (odd year) Fastnet Race always ends on Plymouth Sound in August. On every fourth year, the club's own single-handed race to Newport, Rhode Island, USA, 2,800 nautical miles is run. This is the pioneer race, now widely copied, but still the classic. It is raced every fourth year, 1992, 1996 etc. The two-handed round Britain is held about every four years and calls at Crosshaven, Castle Bay (Outer Hebrides), Lerwick, Lowestoft and back to Plymouth.The two latter races were for years sponsored by the London Sunday newspaper, *The Observer*. In recent years there have been various sponsors for both races.

Members
2,000 men and women. The Patron is HRH Prince Philip. Previous commodores include the then Prince of Wales from 1875 to 1901 and from 1919 to 1935, Winston S. Churchill from 1949 to 1965 and Francis Chichester during 1972.

Address
Queen Anne's Battery, Plymouth, Devon, PL4 0TW, England.
℡ 0752 660077

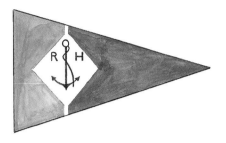

Société des Régates du Havre

This is a senior club in one of France's major Atlantic and Channel ports, Le Havre, and provides a sailing base and meeting place for a catchment area of numerous keen sailors and active socialites. So the membership is large. It was founded in 1838 and the members joke that it is the only 'royal club' in France, as its first president was Louis Philippe, King of the French. Like so many clubs of the Victorian era, its headquarters were originally a big edifice on a seafront; known as the Palais des Régates, this was totally destroyed in 1944 and the present practical building overlooks the yacht harbour. The immediate waters are those of the Baie de la Seine, a big area of fairly sheltered water and the scene of races and yachts on passage throughout the season. Yachts and motor cruisers which intend to cruise up the Seine, or its accompanying canals and waterways, may well come into Le Havre to prepare (lowering masts etc) and then head up the river to Paris.

Out at sea, Le Havre is 100 miles from the Solent with its huge concentration of British yachts, so throughout the season there are always one of more UK flags in view of the club, as well as other nations. It is within a day's sail of many harbours along the French coast to the east and west.

Clubhouse
The clubhouse, overlooking a large marina in the Petit Port right near the entrance to the commercial port, as such, was opened in 1952 (the marina was not there then). In 1972 a major extension of offices, showers and stores was added.

There is a large dining room on the first floor, with the appealing hint of the perfection of food in France and a long bar. These frequently play host to regattas and the finish of races from other harbours in France or from England.

There is hard standing around the club where members work on their boats and a large under cover barn with lockers and space for dinghy and other boat work.

In 1957, just to the east of the old Palais des Régates site, a new building was opened, the large Club-house de Sainte-Adresse. This is a kind of lido for bathing, the beach, diving and board sailing. The club reserves the use of a part of the building which also has indoor sports (table tennis and so on) and a swimming pool.

Waterside
Immediately adjoining the club in the Petit Port is a very large marina. It actually takes an appreciable time to walk along the extensive concrete main fingers from many berths to reach the club. The marina is under the control of the Port of Le Havre. There is virtually always room for visitors. There are other berths in Le Havre in inner basins, some right in the city.

Classes
Cruiser-racers, Laser, 505, Optimist, Snipe.

Events and regattas
The area is a favourite one for the championships of keel-boats and offshore classes. The very first One Ton Cup in offshore boats was held here in 1965 and again in 1967. In racing in the bay, the tidal streams are a major factor and the wind is quite often flukey. The Dragon class is out often in the bay, but is based at Deauville to

the south. British races such as those organized by RORC, JOG and south coast clubs also finish at Le Havre and the club co-operates with the finishing line and crew entertainment.

A strong cruiser element holds regular rallies including one every year at the Royal Lymington Yacht Club. By contrast, board sailing is encouraged and this is conducted off the beach at Sainte-Adresse, where there are also slips for launching small power boats and sailing dinghies. There are small racing dinghies owned by the club for loan to young members.

Members
2,800 : Most of these are resident in or near Le Havre. There are maintained close links with five clubs in England, two in Holland, one in Belgium and one in Switzerland.

Address
Ports des Yachts, Boulevard Clemenceau, 76600 Le Havre, France.

In the city of Le Havre beside the SRH.

Royal Western Yacht Club

Here is a happy club established for over one hundred years, which has never had a clubhouse and with total published assets of about £3,000 ($5,800). A small number of fixtures are run each year with an option for the locality, though this will always be somewhere on the Firth of Clyde. The club's subscription was one guinea from its foundation in 1875 until 1972, when the arrival of decimal currency lowered it to one pound!

History
Twenty-four Scotsmen met at the Waverly Hotel, Glasgow, on 23rd August 1875 to form a club for sailing small yachts and dinghies on the lower Clyde, as existing clubs did not cater for that area. They did not know what to call it, but two months later decided on 'The Western Yacht Club'. In 1885 the club was granted the 'royal' and blue ensign. It remains one of the select list of clubs with the 'blue' undefaced. At the turn of the century, the club ran two racing classes, which appear to have been under some form of restricted rule, being 19ft (5.8m) and 24ft (7.3m) respectively. In 1910, the club ran 'cruising matches' to Tighnabruaich which always ended with a famous party. This race now runs from Gourock and that evening at Tighnabruaich Pier there is still an annual party.

Events and regattas
Kip International Regatta is run in May, then Tighnabruaich, for the Bryce Allan Cup, mentioned above, in July the third main regatta is East Patch regatta in August. There are several permanent trophies. The Etchells 22 nationals were run in 1982 and 1986 off Troon. Thus the club is of an earlier tradition, as can be seen in these pages, where clubs formed in the nineteenth century had small memberships, ran just a few regattas a year and met at places other than a clubhouse. It is pleasing to find such an institution still active, the members today being mainly those who have sailed for a year or two in its regattas. They have an annual dinner in the winter.

Members
369

Address
c/o Hon Secretary, Lochaber, 20 Barclay Drive, Helensburgh, G84 9RB, Scotland.
☎ 0436 72088

Note
Although this is the R Western YC of Scotland, and was founded later than the R Western YC of England, it does not have the extra designation of the country in the title.

Racing in the Kyles of Bute in the Firth of Clyde.

The distinguished and ancient Yorkshire One-Design of the Royal Yorkshire Yacht Club.

Royal Yorkshire Yacht Club

This distinguished club is far from any other, on a long exposed stretch of the coast of Yorkshire facing the North Sea. The town of Bridlington is at least within a bay, protected from the north by the big headland of Flamborough Head and the prevailing south-westerly wind where most, but not all gales come from, blows from off the land. One of the club's classes is the oldest one-design class raced in England.

Clubhouse
The same clubhouse has been occupied since 1900 and remains in a pleasant street in Bridlington, looking over the harbour. It is open all year with dining room, meeting and committee rooms and bedrooms. Visitors from recognized yacht clubs are welcome. Members considered moving to a modern building, but decided in 1991 to refurbish the old house with all its character and launched an appeal accordingly.

Waterside
Bridlington is a drying harbour with a narrow entrance between piers and not accessible at low water. Visiting boats can dry out or lie alongside the quay. There is spacious launching for racing dinghies and catamarans at Blyth Park one mile south of the club and harbour. There are changing rooms, showers and a recreation room with a view of Flamborough Head and the long beach which stretches far south. On the ground is a boat compound, sail store, launch and recovery tractor and race office. Rescue and committee boats are on station. Olympic style courses can be set.

History
The club was founded in 1847. The Yorkshire One-Design class sailed its first season in 1898, ten having been built by Field and Co., Itchen Ferry, Southampton and sent to Bridlington by rail. On arrival lots were drawn to determine the owners and the boats were taken by horse and cart to the harbour. With 3.5ft (1.1m) draught, they took the ground at low water and every Saturday in the season from 1898 to 1900, they raced. The class joined the R Yorkshire YC in 1906 and many years of racing followed. By 1945 only five of the original boats remained; however five new boats were built locally soon after. In 1973, the class converted from gaff to Bermudan rig. In 1992, the class of ten continued to race regularly, four of them being the original 1898 boats. If this is rather more than we have given to other classes, it is surely allowed for the oldest existing one-design in England.

Classes
Yorkshire One-design 25.5ft,(7.8m), J24, National Squib, Cruiser, Dart catamaran.

Events and regattas
The Top Dog Race starts the season; the Gallon Race ends it.

Regatta week, the second week of August. There is a dinghy regatta and a catamaran regatta in mid-June. The Dowsing Trophy is an annual '24-hour race' round the lightship of that name. In 1991 and 1992, the club ran the E-boat nationals. The Royal Jubilee Cup, for the best cruising log.

Members
660

Address
1 Windsor Terrace, Bridlington, Yorkshire, YO15 3HX, England. ✆ 0262 672041

Royal Highland Yacht Club

Well north of the Clyde estuary, north of latitude fifty-six degrees and in reach of the Western Isles and on the edges of the Scottish Highlands, is the town of Oban on the Firth of Lorn. Here until 1946, the Royal Highland Yacht Club had a clubhouse, but since then it has run events and regattas without any permanent base. But its regattas and meets remain centred on these outstandingly beautiful waters.

History

In September 1881, gentlemen from *'leading Highland families'* met in Oban to form a yacht club. Such was the standing of these people that in less than two months the Home Office had obtained the Queen's approval to the title 'royal' and the use of the Blue Ensign. This would be astonishing today.

Following the customs of the day, the members tended to meet on social occasions such as the Oban Games, while holding a single annual regatta on a fixed local course. In 1898 the club bought a house on the front at Oban with a small slipway. Membership at the time was about 200. In 1901, no regatta was held because of the death of the Queen. During the 1930s, no regattas were held by the club and in 1937, the membership stood at 94. In 1940 the clubhouse was taken over by the Royal Air Force and Red Cross and at the end of the war, the clubhouse was sold for £5,369. However the decision was taken to concentrate on sailing fixtures and the first of these took place in August 1947; this later developed into the successful West Highland Week. Activities virtually expanded in line with the general expansion of yachting in the UK and one must remember that the Western Isles are a beautiful cruising ground, without the large local population to supply intense racing. In 1981 there was a centenary regatta.

Classes

Cruiser-racer, Dragon

Events and regattas

West Highland Week remains the main annual event in conjunction with other clubs. There are three summer musters for cruisers and some weekend musters, a fitting-out supper and laying-up supper. The club runs a cruising log competition and there are numerous racing cups.

Members

509

Address

Secretary at West Manse House, Kilchrenan, Taynuilt, Argyll, PA35 1HG, Scotland.
✆ 08663 213

Royal Highland Yacht Club 'muster' at Loch Spelve, Isle of Mull, Argyll.

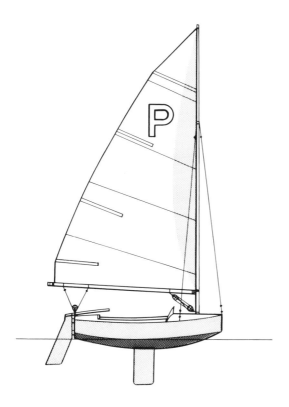

The P-class 7ft (2.1m) wooden one-design is the first boat in the life of many New Zealand sailors, designed seventy years ago.
Some 600 sail regularly.

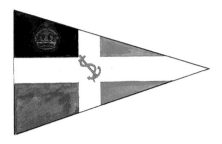

Royal Port Nicholson Yacht Club

This is a principal club in the capital city on the North Island of New Zealand. Wellington has a number of yacht harbours and docks and the RPNYC is in the Clyde Quay Boat Harbour, where there is berthing for more than seventy yachts. This is also convenient to the centre of Wellington, making the club very popular and in the high numbers for club membership. Yet there is also a long history of 110 years.

Clubhouse
The present site was first occupied when the main yachting base in the city became Clyde Quay in 1902. In 1946 a slipway was constructed here, but a few years later it was evident that the old clubhouse was inadequate. For some years this was the outstanding problem for the RPNYC, but in the fifties an existing building constructed by American forces in the war and on the boat harbour, was eventually acquired and after extensive alterations opened as the clubhouse in 1958. In 1983 it was discovered that there was no legal ownership of the building! It was purchased, pulled down and a new clubhouse built; this was opened by the Governor General in 1987. In 1991, an extension in the form of an external timber deck with all weather awning was added.

History
There are records of yachting off Wellington in 1841, but the club was founded in 1883 following a meeting at the Pier Hotel. The Governor General became the commodore and in the early years there were some forty yachts sailing. From then on it was seaworthy cruisers or cruiser-racers that were the main type of vessel. In 1891 a New Zealand Yachting Association was formed with uniform rules for use throughout the country. In 1896 members were permitted to fly the Blue Ensign. The 'royal' title followed in 1921.

The 1960s saw the expansion of ocean racing with the first New Zealand teams in the Sydney-Hobart Race and later in other international offshore events. A senior member and flag officer, Hal Wagstaff, was appointed president of the New Zealand Yachting Federation from 1989 onwards.

Classes
Cruiser-racers

Events and regattas
The cruising section of the club records many voyages including those of long distances. Some 220 yachts are on the list of those owned by members. The club publishes a quarterly magazine which is taken by some 1,500 sailors on top of the club membership. There are a number of other marinas and docks around Wellington, apart from that over which the club has a view. There is a major youth training programme in the club. There are races at weekends and on Wednesday evenings throughout the season using handicap systems , which at present are PHRF and IMS. There is a winter season series on Sundays from early June to mid-August. The club has numerous trophies and cups awarded for different courses and groups of races. There are a number of major and minor social events throughout the year.

Members
1,200. Patron: HE The Governor General.

Address
Clyde Quay Boat Harbour, P.O.Box 9674, Wellington, New Zealand. ✆ 848 700

Koninklijke Zeil-en Roei Veneniging, Hollandia

Literally the 'royal sail and rowing club', this club calls itself the Royal Yacht Club Hollandia. It was established in 1882 and was based in Rotterdam.

Clubhouse
The clubhouse was built in a new site altogether after World War II for active sailing at Braassemermeer. With the completion of the IJsselmeer, recovered from the old Zuyder Zee, the club moved in 1963 to the small town of Medemblik. The clubhouse is essentially a sailing station and is closed in the winter.

Classes
Olympic classes

Events and regattas
Like a number of yacht clubs, the activities changed considerably in recent years, a long established and social club taking on a new role. In this case the move to Medemblik, made it an ideal base for dinghy and keel-boat sailing on Olympic type courses and in this the club has been a world leader. Every year, there are one or more world championships. Also every year, at least since 1985, there has been a regatta for all Olympic classes. The IYRU has used the club in the past for major trials of new classes; for instance the two-man keel-boat was chosen there in 1965.

More recent championships have been:1990 Soling, Tornado, 470-men, 470-women worlds, Solo worlds; 1993 Contender worlds, H-Boat worlds.

Members
800

Address
Clubhouse: Oosterhaven, Medemblik. Secretary: Mrs M. Pannevis, Schiedamseweg 5, 3026AA, Rotterdam, Netherlands.
℡ 010 4766380

Each boat is welcomed at the end of the annual 24-hour race at Medemblik.

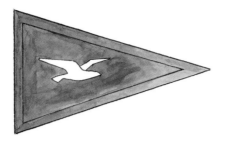

Thorpe Bay Yacht Club

On an unusual stretch of the coast of England where low tide reveals miles of sand flats, while the shore is heavily built up with both industry and the resort of Southend-on-Sea, (founded for the working people of the east-end of London), hundreds of boats and yachts are based. It is the north shore of the Thames Estuary on the shipping route into London.

The *Guinness Book of Records* gives Southend Pier as the longest in the world at 2,150 metres (Since 1889 it has been breached by fourteen vessels and had three major fires). To the east of it, where dried-out sailing and motor boats lie on the sands, the residential areas become more prosperous, the shore has a shallow indentation and Thorpe Bay Yacht Club is conspicuous.

Clubhouse
Suburbia runs right to the beach, but the club, a two-storey building, is one road back, Thorpe Bay Gardens, from the seafront on rising ground, so the effect is to look straight out to the drying moorings and the extent of the Thames Estuary. When built, the ground was farm land. There is a peculiar satisfaction in having this large building among the residential area and its nearby shops and resort.

It is surrounded by laying up space and car parking. On the beach in front is an old hut used as bosun's store and race box: before 1959 this was the actual 'clubhouse'. In the present clubhouse there are a dining room and two bars on the first floor; one can be used for those who want more quiet than is sometimes acceptable to the young and active membership. The ground floor has offices, changing rooms and the steward's flat.

Waterside
There are 140 moorings which are afloat for six hours on every tide, but most of which dry out at low water. This area of water is reserved to the club and its members. These comprise Sandhoppers, sailing cruisers, motor boats and club rescue boats. The club's own slipway by the huts on the beach is used for launching dinghies from the boat park.

The mooring area is exposed, but the prevailing wind is from up the Thames. In the 'hurricane' of October 1987, every single vessel on a mooring, ended up on the beach, with varying degrees of damage. In the club are photographs of this – it is hoped, isolated – event.

History
This is one of those clubs resulting from a schism. In 1949, a number of members of the Thames Estuary Yacht Club, led by Kit Hobday, met in the beach hut and formed the club. Immediately among the members were keen racing men and the open water in full view of the beach meant that dinghy championships and Olympic courses were a major activity. On several occasions British trials for the smaller classes in Olympic Games took place there. Varnished wooden boards in the bar show the Olympic feats of members in the Flying Dutchman and Finn classes in the 1964 Games in Tokyo. Increasing specialization of all classes means that this aspect of racing has given way to other kinds. One or more national championships for dinghy classes are held off the club, almost every year; for instance, the Moth class in 1992 and Albacore class in 1993.

The view at low tide from Thorpe Bay Yacht Club.

Classes
Sandhopper, cruiser-racer, Laser, Mirror, Optimist, Topper, dinghy handicap using Portsmouth Yardstick.

Events and regattas
The club is typical of scores around the coasts of England in that every weekend and on midweek evenings as well, regular racing is clocked up around the club's buoys. Starting in mid-March with the warm-up series, the races go through summer, then autumn and winter series until just before Christmas. Like many other clubs, there is no major agreement on a single dinghy class and handicap racing is the usual system, with the help of the long established Portsmouth Yardstick.

Interspersed among the weekly racing are trophies created by the club with names like the Benfleet Shield (a race to Benfleet Creek, 'weather permitting') and the Kit Hobday Anniversary Trophy. Then there are the Veterans' Cup, the Frozen Sheets Trophy and the Ladies Race Trophy, which describe themselves.

The Sandhopper, designed locally by Oliver Lee, as the most numerous single class, has its own additional fixtures for longer distances (to neighbouring creeks, for instance). Races for slightly larger cruisers go further up the English coast, into London itself and on a summer rally to France.

The spacious club building provides opportunity for social events. These are based around prize givings, class suppers, championship programmes; also Christmas and new year parties when for a few weeks no sailing is organized. There is an annual ball each November.

Members
753

Address
115 Thorpe Bay Gardens, Thorpe Bay, Southend-on-Sea, Essex, SS1 3NW, England.
✆ 0702 587563

Royal Artillery Yacht Club

There are numerous sailing clubs in the British Navy, Army and Air Force. The British Army is traditionally split into many regiments in which men and women spend their entire careers, so there are separately established clubs for Armoured Corps, Corps of Transport, Engineers as well as clubs long established on station: British Berlin YC, British Dummersee YC, British Forces SA (Hong Kong), Inter-Services YC, Episkopi (Cyprus).

Rather more starchy however, were older clubs originally formed for officers only, of whom a high proportion owned their own vessels. One of these is the Royal Artillery Yacht Club.

Clubhouse

As a world wide club for active sailors, there has never been any call for a single clubhouse. Any funds available go into boats and events.

History

As horsemanship and riding were central to the sporting values of officers of the Royal Artillery in 1933, the appointment of a commodore, Colonel Arthur Main, who was a fine horseman, on the formation of the Royal Artillery Yacht Club on 16th June that year, was important in the club's initial credibility.

By 1939, there were 455 members, thirteen club yachts and sixty-six private yachts. The club boats were in fact small racers and keel-boats in several stations around the coasts of England and also at Aden, Bombay, Gibraltar, Manora (Karachi) and Malta.

Meanwhile in 1936, the club had been given an 1899 gaff yawl as an ocean racer, which did well in RORC Class B (for older yachts) in the three pre-war seasons from 1937. After being hit by an incendiary bomb in 1943, she was sold for £475. In 1948, the club built its own 51ft (15.5m) ocean racer; she was called *St Barbara*, who is the patron saint of gunners. Many successful seasons of ocean racing, regatta racing and cruising followed. (She was finally sold out of the club to a private owner in 1966). The club also had permanent use of the ex-German 50 square metres *Brunhilde* (re-named *Brynmere*) and *Seefalke* (re-named *Sea Falcon*). Another 50 square, *Rosanna*, was stationed in Tripoli and Malta.

By 1969, the club had 1,000 members and an extensive club-owned fleet of offshore yachts, dinghies and other racing boats. There were annual regattas and all kinds of competitions, including matches against other service clubs and associations. There was regular traffic of yachts between England and the army bases in the Baltic, where some club boats were sailed all season.

In the 1970s competition in RORC racing for service manned yachts was becoming difficult because of the increasing cost, professionalism and rapid design replacement. The RAYC more than made up for this by engaging in the wider range of races available and voyaging its offshore and cruising fleet to Russia, the USA, the Mediterranean and elsewhere. For the US bicentenary in 1976, the club manned the Army Nicholson 55, *Sabre*, which voyaged to the 4th July water parade and also to Newport RI, where the US artillery gave her a warm welcome.

By the 80s, there had been *St Barbaras II*,

III and *IV*, the latter being a Nicholson 40 cruiser-racer, while *II* was a an old Rebel design kept in Germany. All ranks were now eligible for membership and all kinds of trophies, fixtures and sailing qualifications were operating every year.

Events and regattas

Annual regattas for dinghies (typical venue: Whale island), keel-boats (Seaview), cruiser-racers (Yarmouth, IOW); participation by club teams in Army Sailing Association annual fixtures. Commodore's Cup for races representing club groups, units and headquarters. Numerous other trophies.

Classes

Club owns five cruiser-racers 32 to 40 ft; ten Enterprise dinghies. Extensive use made of Army boats and other boats from helpful clubs for inter-unit etc racing.

Members

1,400. The flag officers are invariably Colonels, Brigadiers and Generals.

Address

Hon Secretary, Royal Artillery Yacht Club, RSA, Larkhill, Salisbury, Wiltshire SP4 8QT, England.

St Barbara (dark spinnaker), club yacht of the Royal Artillery YC for many years, races past HMS *Vanguard*, the last British battleship.

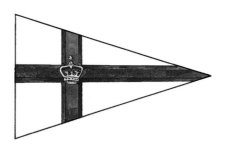

Royal Burnham Yacht Club

In England (not Scotland or Ireland), although all kinds of sailing are widespread, there are two areas which are considered the prime ones for yacht racing. These are the Solent area and the coast of Essex. The latter is not only near London, but is close to the birth of English yachting, being in effect an extension of the Thames Estuary and was traditionally the site of some of the great yacht builders in wood and the source of professional yacht crews (in past days – fishing in winter, yachting in summer). The most intense racing base in Essex is the River Crouch and its town of Burnham, which boasts a number of yacht clubs in sight of one another: the Burnham Sailing Club, the Crouch Yacht Club, the Royal Corinthian Yacht Club and the Royal Burnham Yacht Club.

Clubhouse

The buildings along the waterfront at Burnham-on-Crouch are continuous, but always behind the high sea wall, which gives a walk for several miles along the river bank. One complex of these, obviously altered and extended over the years is the clubhouse. There is a dining room, ballroom and members' rooms as well as a most competent starting box over one of the roofs. Among these structures is the original building of 1895. Part of the facade has changed little since then and there was even a 'look-out platform on the roof'. Have watchers become soft, or is that today people are not ashamed to make themselves more comfortable with better protection (or did they and do we just ape ship's bridges of the respective periods)?.

In 1923 there was apparently a former pickle factory (that is how it is described) next door and this was acquired to extend the clubhouse. There were added two-room apartments, bathrooms, steward's quarters and a bicycle shed. The next year an extra kitchen was put in and other improvements and the clubhouse became responsible for hoisting visual gale warnings (north and south cones) when the coastguard at Walton-on-Naze sent through a message.

By 1936 there was a tennis court at the back, while a major part of the club was, as it had always been, for men only. In 1973 there was a fire which destroyed the ballroom and a number of the flats. Over the next decade rebuilding took place to give a combination of accommodation for members and new flats which were leased for the financial benefit of the club.

Not many clubs have remained in the same buildings for so long, but the site of the Royal Burnham looking over the Crouch with its hundreds of moorings, would be needed as a yacht club, if there was not one there already.

Waterside

A floating jetty runs out from the sea wall in front of the club. This was opened by the former Prime Minister, Edward Heath, in April 1975. From there the club launches take members out to their boats which are customarily on swinging moorings. Ten small yachts and keel-boats can lie there for short periods. However since 1985 a large marina was created about one mile upriver from the club, giving members all the advantages without having actually to see it from the veranda!

Centre of activity at England's major east coast yachting port,
the Royal Burnham Yacht Club.

History

The story of the actual clubhouse is told above. In the nineteenth century, Burnham was an isolated fishing village, though agricultural products were also sent from there to London by sea. A line of the Great Eastern Railway arrived at Burnham in 1889, connecting it with Liverpool Street station, London. The Royal Corinthian moved to Burnham from the too-commercial Thames in 1893, as did the London Sailing Club (no longer extant). The first Burnham Week (see below) took place in 1893 with races for 1 raters, half raters and cruisers.

Then apparently some cruising men felt the need of a club. Among those who formed the Burnham Yacht Club, which opened on Easter Saturday, 13th April 1895, was an Italian, Eugene de Pallas, who was the prime mover and first honorary secretary. Strangely the first club burgee consisted of the Italian national colours with a badge.

In those days, racing was not thought proper on Sundays, while the members from London usually worked in their offices on Saturday mornings. This made racing rather like the modern mid-week evening race! An early dispute was amateur versus professional, when a paid skipper took the helm during a club race; the problem was difficult to solve.

By 1914, the Crouch Yacht Club having been formed in 1907, the river was acknowledged as one of the leading regatta ports, comparable with Cowes and the Clyde. This was partly due to yachting being driven out of its place of origin, the London River, by the particularly grimy face of Victorian and Edwardian commerce. All today's clubs were there except for the Burnham Sailing Club which appeared in 1930. There were also the United Hospitals Sailing Club and London Sailing Club, which have since moved away. Unusually, by that time the club had redesigned its burgee no less than three times, dropping the Italian colours in 1898, then changing again in 1905 and 1913, the latest showing the shield of the county of Essex. A fifth burgee dropped this in 1928, when the club became 'royal' and put a crown in the middle of the blue and red cross on white. The correspondence involved with the royal warrant was quite extensive, this being perhaps the period when such matters had become pompous and time consuming, well after the time when 'royals' were handed out to clubs with some ease and before later years, when such titles are seldom, if ever granted. The club was allowed to use a blue ensign with simply a crown on it, which was counted a considerable privilege.

In the late thirties, both sailing and the social aspects increased. For instance the club had winter balls at London hotels such as the Mayfair and Dorchester with a titled and beribboned guest list. Membership in 1939 was 450.

In the second world war, sailing continued for a brief time above a boom across the mouth of the Crouch, but later the clubhouse became part of HMS *St Matthew*, a base for landing training, the navy making some changes to the interior of the club. After 1945, the sailing and racing became intense. The story of the club virtually is that of the leading edge of post-war racing in England. In particular club members were involved in the growth of ocean and passage racing and it would be invidious to pick out names. In 1950, it was one of the participating clubs in the formation of the East Anglian Offshore Racing Association (EAORA), now a leading organizer of races of over fifty miles all through the season.

Burnham Week, at the end of August/beginning of September thrived annually with ocean racing classes, keel-boats and dinghies. The club was the challenging club for the British boat, *Victory 83*, owned by Peter de Savary, in the *America*'s Cup trials and races of 1983. The 12-metre got as far as the final round for challenges, but was there beaten in all races except one by the outstanding *Australia II*

with her innovative wing keel and which went on to win the cup itself.

It is said, not entirely seriously, that the real hard-tack sailors of England are those of the estuaries among the flat Essex and Suffolk marshes, rather than the populated south coast, for all its number of yachting events.

Classes

Cruiser-racer (rated by RORC Channel Handicap System), Dragon, Squib, Sonata, Scow, Royal Burnham One-Design.

In May 1925, the West Solent Restricted class, a 34ft (10.4m) keel-boat was adopted for the club. Shortly after two other small keel-boats, which died out in the 1950s were in use, the East Coast OD and the Crouch OD. The West Solent disappeared after 1940. The Royal Burnham One-Design was started in 1932 and was built by King and Son, a Burnham builder (in wood, of course). Nine were immediately ordered. There are now about twenty-two racing regularly.

Events and regattas

Burnham Week (in conjunction with other Burnham clubs and the town) with about 420 starters each day in twenty-seven classes and in England, second only to Cowes as a regatta week. Always held over what is now the late August public holiday. Cadet Week, EAORA Ralph Herring race offshore, weekend racing for all courses. Summer Ball, New Year's Eve Ball.

The EAORA inter-club championship has been won by club in a number of years

Members

750. Patron since 1952 HRH Prince Philip. Leading yachtsmen members: Sir Edward Heath, Sir Maurice Laing, Ron Amey, David Edwards, R.C.Watson - all leading figures in British ocean racing between 1960 and 1980.

Address

The Quay, Burnham-on-Crouch, Essex, CM0 8AU, England.
✆ 0621 782044

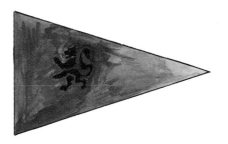

London Corinthian Sailing Club

A number of yacht clubs have evacuated from the waterways of big cities, especially near the beginning of this century as industrialization and pollution of the water increased. Among these have been the Royal London Yacht Club (from London to Cowes), the Royal Southern YC (from Southampton to Hamble) and the New York Yacht Club (whose racing courses moved from Manhattan to Long Island Sound and Newport). The London Corinthian is one which has returned to a location near the centre of a metropolis from its outer locality at Burnham-on-Crouch, where it was giving races before the existing Burnham clubs were established. Three years after the railway line was built from London to Burnham, in summer 1892, the club gave a regatta: it was the first Burnham Week. The club was then called the London Sailing Club and the first commodore was George Terrell; the name is apparently still well known around the River Crouch.

Clubhouse
The old clubhouse was demolished in 1964 to allow for the expansion, after a use of eighty years, of Furnival Gardens beside the River Thames. The club moved to the present Linden House, a listed Georgian building. As well as occupying this, accommodation for over 100 boats was constructed indoors and outside below a new development of apartments. The ground floor of Linden House has a ballroom for 100 people, a Captain's room for small meetings and lectures; the first floor has another similar meeting room, a sizeable bar and the kitchen, as well as the club offices. In the basement are changing rooms.

The clubhouse is only a few minutes walk from the Great West Road, on which traffic pours day and night in and out of London, yet its riverside situation makes one unaware of the urban surroundings.

Waterside
On the river bank there is a race officers' box for control, starts and finishes. Close to it are two launching pontoons. This part of the river Thames is under the control of Thames Conservancy, an agency with considerable powers and it is patrolled by the water-borne arm of the Metropolitan Police.

History
In 1894 the Royal Corinthian YC became involved in the Burnham Regatta, it too being a club on the already heavily commercial Thames. The London Sailing Club continued to give an annual regatta at Burnham for some years, but a part of the club moved to a permanent clubhouse in Furnival gardens in west London on the river Thames about five miles upstream from London Bridge. This became known as the London Corinthian Sailing Club. Later, the members who had been resident at Burnham were absorbed into the Royal Corinthian, which moved there. From its inception the LCSC was one of the three or four clubs within London which uninterruptedly gave small boat sailing in the heavily built up area on either side of the Thames.

It came into its own in World War II when all sailing and boating was prohibited around the coasts of Great Britain. Suitable inland waters were exempt and the London Corinthian Yacht Club continued to give races using craft such as the United

Hospitals dinghy, a typical 14ft (4.3m) clinker wood centreboarder of the time. For instance in April 1942, when the war was raging around the globe, *'assorted craft including 14ft Internationals competed in a strong westerly wind in one long round between Hammersmith and Barnes Bridges'*. Nearby clubs active in this way in the war, were the Minima Yacht Club and the Ranelagh Sailing Club, which *'provided diversion for active members of HM services including New Zealand naval officers who were well known yachtsmen there'*. In June 1943, the 'Annual Invitation Handicap' was held between the same bridges and prizes were presented by Petty Officer A.P.Herbert MP (famous in his time as a champion of the London River, a humorous author and poet and today for his battle to establish authors' lending rights). As the war ended this part of the river became a pioneer in the development of new light modern racing dinghies for post-war sailing.

Classes
International 14 footer, National Enterprise, International Laser, Laser 2, dinghy handicap.

Events and regattas
The courses are set between Hammersmith Bridge and Barnes Bridge. Summer (April to September) racing is every weekend and certain evening. Winter racing is every other weekend. There is no gap between the two. One fixture is *'25th December Christmas day sailing - no rescue boat'*! However the boat returns for *' 26th December Christmas Punch Bowl Handicap'*

Main social events are the Summer Ball and Annual Prize giving. Numerous cups are fitted around weekend racing. The club shows on its race card for the whole year, the name of the race officer for every race. If a race officer is missing, the whole club knows who it is, one system of ensuring attendance.

Dinghy class championships are invariably held on the sea in the summer as holiday weeks, so such fixtures are never held at the London Corinthian, which is there to serve a different purpose. Members trail their racing dinghies to the coast for championships, but can use them during the week a few minutes after leaving an office in the centre of a huge urban area.

Members
350 : The most notable president of the club was A.P.Herbert (see above).

Address
Linden House, Upper Mall, Hammersmith, London, W6 9TA, England.
℗ 081 748 3280

Facing the River Thames for dinghy sailing, the long established London Corinthian YC.

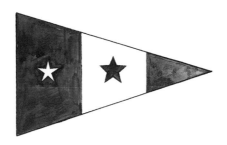

Yacht Club de France

In a volume the size of a paperback novel and with 244 pages, the 1932 handbook of the Yacht Club de France was an impressive work of reference. The patron was the President of the Republic; presidents of honour were the Ministers of the Marine and Marine Marchande; vice presidents were a deputy MP, a Vice-Admiral and a Baron.

Since the previous century the club by its very name had been the senior one in France and, whatever its activities, has always had its headquarters in Paris, inevitable in one the world's most centrist of countries.

Clubhouse

The club has rooms just off the Champs Elysée with a library, dining room and offices. In the earliest days the club had rooms in first one building and then another, starting at 18 rue de Berlin on 31st July 1867, then moving in 1868, 1872 and 1898. From then for many years the club was in the first floor of 82 boulevard Haussmann, until finally moving to 6 rue Galilée in 1968 and subsequently to the present location in 1991.

History

There were earlier clubs in France than the Yacht Club de France itself. The club at Le Havre was formed in 1838 (page 21) and the Cercle de la Voile de Paris started in 1858. However there was a parallel move to run races and work out handicaps at sailing stations along the River Seine at Argenteuil, Bougival, Suresnes and Joinville; in a word, there seemed a need for central organization, there being no concept in any country of a national authority in the current sense. The people working these things out called themselves the Société des Régates Parisiennes and in June 1867 formed the Société d'Encouragement pour la Navigation de Plaisance. However on 11th November at a meeting in the Ministry for the Marine, the name was changed to the Yacht Club de France. An Admiral was the first president (the word president is the French usage; the Anglo-American commodore is not used).

Two details are significant. The club was officially created in effect by the state, or at least under its authority. Secondly, after the earlier organizations had used words like 'Société' and 'Cercle', the chosen description became the English words 'Yacht Club' (de France): the very phrase created in England in 1815. (page 16). The Société d'Encouragement has remained a description or sub-title to this day, to which is added 'Reconnue d'Utlité Publique par Decrét du 30 Juillet 1914'. At least the first two presidents were Admirals in the Marine.

In 1886 a rival organization, the UYF, was instrumental in bringing in a series of tonnage classes under a new rating rule. They were grouped as 3 to 5 tons, 5 to 10 and so on and there were time allowances. It was a time also in America and England when rating rules were going through a controversial and rapidly changing period.

In 1891 the club created the Coupe de France; six years later that 'became international' when it was won by the Royal Temple YC (page 136); since then it has been sailed in various classes in Europe more than fifty times. In 1902 as the rating rules of UYF crumbled, it was absorbed into YCF. Then in 1906 and 1907, international conferences were called in London and Paris, to unify the racing (right of way) and rating (yacht

Coupe de France,
one of the world's great yachting prizes.

measurement and time allowance) rules. The YCF was the body which represented France. An international yacht racing union was formed to administer these rules with the secretariat in England, but on the permanent committee of five men, the French had M. Le Bret of 57 avenue d'Antin, Paris. In 1938, a conventional sailing authority for all French yacht clubs was formed, the USNF, later the FFYV and now the FFV.

In 1940 the club membership stood at 870 and 418 yachts, and after World War II, despite the difficulties, some 808 old or new members immediately renewed their membership. By 1957, it was up to 950 members and 460 yachts; by 1967, 1,096 members and 575 yachts and it had acquired a small additional clubhouse at St Tropez.

Until 1970, the *America*'s Cup was an Anglo-Saxon monopoly (USA, Britain, Australia and Canada), but the Yacht Club de Hyères challenged in the person of Baron Bic in the 12-metre class. The YCF first challenged in 1983 being duly eliminated in challengers' trials at Newport, RI. It challenged again at San Diego in 1992 in the very large new IACC (International *America*'s Cup Class). A massive effort under Marc

Pajot went into this campaign with the yacht *Ville de Paris*, which was eliminated before the final challenger round.

Events and regattas
Social occasions in Paris and patronage of French sailing initiatives on many occasions. The 'Coupe de France' was for many years awarded to the 8-metre class and subsequently the 5.5-metre class; it has since been re-allocated for the Dragon class.

Members
1,500: Most leading French sailors are members as well as being members of their local or original clubs. Past members include Jean Charcot, the polar explorer, Mme Virginie Hériot, who had a series of successes in racing including the 1928 Olympic Games, Alain Gerbault one of the early round the world navigators, Marin-Marie, another single-handed sailor and sea painter and today Eric Tabarly.

Address
4 rue Chalgrin, 75116 Paris, France
✆ 01033 1 45 01 28 46

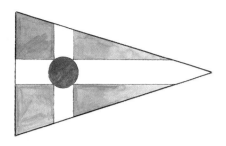

Yokohama Yacht Club

Yacht racing and yacht clubs are an 'imported culture' according to a Japanese correspondent, though that comment could apply to many countries, perhaps even all outside England and the Netherlands! In 1913 a book was published in Yokohama, Japan. It was called *The Venturesome Voyages of Captain Voss*: it became one of the most famous yacht voyaging books ever. Captain Voss built the 25ft (7.6m) *Sea Queen* in Yokohama and set sail from there on 27th July 1912. The evening before *'all three of the crew being members of the Yokohama Yacht Club, we were honoured with a farewell dinner by members of that organization'*. *Sea Queen* famously ran into a typhoon, which caused severe destruction on the coast of Japan.

Clubhouse

Following the purchase of the club land to construct an elevated motor expressway, the club moved upstream to new land of 660 square metres and put in hand new club premises.

Waterside

Yokohama, opened to the outside world in 1859 at the end of Japan's centuries of isolation, has a massive turnover of trade and shipping. As part of the Yokohama 21st Century Project, two sizeable marinas have been completed in the 1990s: each has capacity for about 1,600 yachts.

History

The club was in at the very beginnings of yachting in Japan, probably because of the presence of Europeans trading in the port. In 1886 the Yokohama Amateur Rowing Club was formed, which became the Yokohama Sailing Club and in 1896, the Yokohama Yacht Club. The aim was then yacht racing and social activities were not permitted. Meanwhile in 1893, an Englishman, Henry Cooke, introduced yacht design and building by opening a boat yard on the edge of the foreign settlement of Yokohama. He taught a Japanese, Tomokazu Okamoto. The yard today is the Okamoto Shipyard, whose retired president is Yutaka Okamoto, son of Tomokazu. 100 years later he is a leading yachtsman and ex-commodore of the Yokohama YC. At the turn of the century, it broadened out into a sports club being incorporated as a Shadan Hojin, which means a non-profit making body to serve the public interest. Swimming, tennis and other sport were included as well as yacht racing.

In 1923, most of Yokohama was destroyed by earthquake, but early recovery of the club was assisted by a new class of racing 18 footers (5.5m), built by the yard. In 1930, the Yokohama Sailing Club was formed and raced with and against the Yokohama YC, which remained all foreign. In 1936, Japan entered her first ever boats in the Olympic Games at Kiel, in preparation for the games of 1940, which never took place.

The story gets a bit hazy until the 1960s, when membership was still non-Japanese and had deteriorated to about 80 persons. Membership was then opened to the Japanese, native membership increasing for the 1964 Olympics in Japan and thereafter with more Japanese in 1970. From the late 70s sailing activities improved in modern production boats combined with better berthing facilities available in the Yokohama Citizens' Yacht harbour at Isogo.

Events and regattas

The Yokohama YC has regular racing and junior instruction, as do a number of other clubs in Japan, but remains notable for its early formation. Other clubs are Enoshima YC, host to the 1964 Olympic Games; Fukuoka YC, joint organizer of the Auckland-Fukuoka Race; Hiroshima YC, host of Hawaii-Hiroshima ('Remember Pearl Harbor to No More Hiroshima'); Hayama Marina YC, host of the Nippon Cup match racing; Kansai YC, major player in Osaka-Kobe waters.

Members
500

Address
Yokohama, Japan.

The clubhouse of the Yokohama Yacht Club today, with a large area around it for hauling out.

Royal Sydney Yacht Squadron

Within what is billed as the world's largest natural harbour, Sydney, New South Wales, Australia, a number of yacht clubs co-ordinate their race programmes. Among these leading clubs of Sydney are the Cruising Yacht Club of Australia (page 86), the Middle Harbour Yacht Club, the Sydney Amateur Sailing Club, the Royal Prince Alfred Yacht Club, Royal Prince Edward Yacht Club and the Royal Sydney Yacht Squadron. With the RYS (page 63) and the Royal New Zealand Yacht Squadron, it uses, rather than 'club' the designation 'squadron'. In each case this is of historical significance only and the function is comparable with any other club. As is the case in many Australian clubs, ladies are not admitted as members but can become associate members. Except for the associate and junior committees, all the main committees are men only. Activities patronized by associates include bridge teams, visits to the Sydney playhouse, the annual luncheon and a cruise around the harbour – by ferry boat! An annual report states that 'many of our associates own or sail yachts'. This view of women is almost unique to Australia.

Clubhouse
This is a building dating from 1840 at Milsons Point overlooking the harbour. It has a dining room, bar and club offices and eight bedrooms for use by members.

Waterside
There is hardstanding for forty-five yachts and four short stay moorings. The adjoining marina has ninety berths; there is dinghy launching. Like a number of enlightened clubs, a boat maintenance and repair firm is alongside and owned by the club: Careel Boat Services Pty.

History
In June 1862, *Chance*, a schooner of 71 tons owned by the Honourable William Walker of the Royal Thames Yacht Club, London, arrived in Sydney. Walker came to settle and trade in Australia.

On 8th July 1862, nineteen yachtsmen of Sydney met in the office at the Exchange Building, of William Walker and resolved *'We, the undersigned yacht owners, hereby constitute ourselves into a club to be termed The Australian Yacht Squadron'*. Less than a year later the club had become the Royal Sydney Yacht Squadron, with patron, HRH The Prince of Wales on the recommendation of the Secretary of State for the Colonies, the Duke of Newcastle.

Walker was commodore from 1862 to 1867. In 1902 the present clubhouse and site were leased to a company owned by the club; later the whole property was purchased by the club. In 1972, the club company changed its name to the same as that of the club and absorbed the club, thus making it a limited company by guarantee.

Classes
Cruiser-racer and offshore racer (in conjunction with other Sydney clubs) handicap by IOR and PHS (equals CHS in Europe). International Dragon, International Etchells 22, International J24, International Yngling, International Laser, Folkboat.

Events and regattas
Annual Squadron May cruise, Sydney

Harbour Regatta, Christmas regatta, Autumn regatta, Australian class championships, spring, summer, main season and winter points series for all classes. Trans Tasman Challenge Cup, inshore races versus RNZYS, Sydney to Gold Coast Race, Sydney to Lord Howe Island. Junior sailing programme with racing against other clubs. Koonya Cup awarded for most outstanding passage in a season.

Members
1,800 : Patron HRH Prince Philip; Commodore-in-Chief His Excellency the Governor-General of Australia.

Address
PO Box 484, Milsons Point, New South Wales 2061, Australia.
℅ 02 955 7171

The imposing battlements of the Royal Sydney Yacht Squadron at Milsons Point which overlook the waters of Sydney Harbour.

The RSYC Crest.

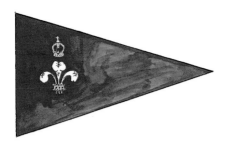

Royal Norfolk and Suffolk Yacht Club

This traditional club with its long built clubhouse, stands right on the easternmost shore of Britain in the town of Lowestoft. The two words are ancient county names from the days of the Anglo-Saxons (in AD 500, 'north and south folk'). The prevailing wind is from the west, so the club has long been host to regattas for boats of all sizes. The large clubhouse in an outer harbour is a few minutes sail from the open sea.

Clubhouse
The prominent clubhouse was built specifically for this club in 1902, the cost being borne by the Great Eastern Railway Company, then the owners of the harbour and then rented to the club on favourable terms. This was perhaps an early form of sponsorship, with some self interest as yachtsmen then used the railway to travel to and from Lowestoft. In 1959, the club purchased the premises from the then British Transport Commission.

There are large public rooms in the Edwardian style with a particularly vast painting of King Edward VII, whose *Britannia* often sailed in the club's regattas. A speciality in this fishing port is kippers (smoked herring) for breakfast.

Waterside
As the clubhouse is in a non tidal outer basin of Lowestoft harbour, there are numerous fore and aft moorings off the club for members and some for visitors. Access is by dinghy pontoon and dinghy. Although the harbour in general is medium size with commercial use, it is exposed in strong winds from the east, a very strong tidal stream can run past the narrow entrance and the banks immediately offshore are shallow in places. However the prevailing wind as already mentioned above alleviates these difficulties.

History
The club as the Norfolk and Suffolk Yacht Club, was formed in 1859 in an effort to regulate the behaviour of sailors on regatta days, especially after an incident the previous year when crews had boarded each other and fought to settle their differences. The club began with fifty-two sailing and forty-two non-sailing members. Like so many of these early clubs, the main events were an annual regatta and meetings in local hostelries. In 1885 the first clubhouse was built on the present site. When it was replaced by the present clubhouse, described above, the old building was moved to the ground of Lowestoft Town Football Club, where it remained until 1990 as a pavilion.

When the Prince of Wales became the patron of the club in 1867, the club changed its flags to show the Prince of Wales feathers and promptly ran into trouble with the Admiralty. Ten years later permission was granted to use the royal feathers and a further ten years passed before the title royal was allowed and a crown added to give the current burgee with a crown over the feather and princely coronet. There it is, with no connection with Norfolk or Suffolk!

Sailing by the club's members was not only on the sea, but also in the large salt water lakes known as 'broads'. Waveney and Oulton Broads are particularly suitable for sailing and racing. The backbone of racing for the first half of the 20th century was in the

Clubhouse and harbour.

Broads One-Design, created by leading members of the club.

Two other classes are particularly associated with this club. The International 14 footers originated by combining Norfolk 14 footers with other classes. The combined class held its first ever championship in 1927; then its second at the club in 1928. Since then many of these Prince of Wales Cups have been held off Lowestoft. The International Dragon class was established at Lowestoft in 1938 and the club has always been a stronghold in England; many of its championships have been held there.

Classes
International Dragon, International Flying 15, National Squib, Broads One-Design, Cruiser-racer (Portsmouth Yardstick).

Events and regattas
Weekend racing for all classes from mid-April to early October. Typical championships sailed during the season are east coast Dragons, National dinghy classes and the main club regatta 'sea week' in early August. Every fourth year the club is a busy host as a finish and restart to the Royal Western Yacht Club round Britain and Ireland two-handed race, the last leg being from Lowestoft to Plymouth.

Members
580 : Edward Heath, ex-prime minister, was a member, as have been for many years individuals from the Coleman family, well known in Norfolk. For many years *Crossbow*, owned by Tim Coleman, held the world sailing speed record for 'large' vessels over 500 metres. There have been fifty-nine commodores since 1859.

Address
Royal Plain, Lowestoft, Suffolk, NR33 0AQ, England.
✆ 0502 566726

Queen Mary Sailing Club

Fifteen miles from the very centre of London (Buckingham palace and the West End) is a complex of reservoirs in the same general area as Heathrow Airport. One of the spreads of water of 700 acres goes by the name of Queen Mary Reservoir: the name of the sailing club follows. Because the surface is raised 45 feet (13.7m) above the surrounding land, the winds are unusually dependable. As well as all the year round racing, the nature and position of the club means there is strong emphasis on training, non-member participation in dinghies, multihulls and board sailors.

Clubhouse
The building, designed for the purpose, dates from 1972 and contains all facilities expected for a dinghy club with starting box and look-out on its own third storey. A crèche is available on Sundays.

Waterside
Slipways for multiple launching descend into the water by the club. On the immediate hardstanding, there is space for 700 boats and a further 240 racks for sailboards. Keel-boats are also kept ashore and are moved by a motorized hoist.

History
Once the water authorities had cleared reservoirs for sailing after World War II, the use of them spread, becoming a rush in the 1960s with the huge expansion of racing and cruising. The club has built up its own traditions in the way of certain fixtures (below) to which sailors come from all over the UK.

Classes
Keel-boats: Flying Fifteen, Yeoman. Dinghies: Contender, Enterprise, Fireball, 505, 420, 470, Merlin-Rocket, Mirror, Laser, Laser 2, Optimists, Tasar, Topper, Sailboards. Other classes sail at open or special events.

Events and regattas
The Bloody Mary each January is a major British dinghy meeting which reached 500 starters in 1989 and is claimed as the world's largest sailing dinghy race. All classes take part using Portsmouth Yardstick. International 14 ft Supercup. National Youth Match racing finals. Queen Mary Marython (best distance after board sailing for three hours).

Weekend racing for class and handicap boats throughout the year. Evening racing on Wednesdays and Thursdays in the summer. Race courses used include Olympic triangle, new Olympic course, fixed-time handicap and pursuit.

Cruising in dinghies is not discouraged, as despite the surrounding urban districts, the waters are quiet and a home for the Grey Heron and other migrating birds.

Training facilities: these are exceptional and the club has been declared a 'centre of excellence' by the national authority. Courses include Learn to Sail, Try Sailing, Seamanship, Refresher Days, Start to Race, High Performance Tuition and many others concerning instructors, catamarans, boards, power-boats, also junior and teenage sessions of all sorts.

Annual Commodore's dinner/dance. Christmas luncheon.

Unusually for a sailing club, dinghies can

be chartered. The club has a red flag flying when 'strong winds are expected'. The club says 'do not regard the red flag as a challenge'!

Members
1,000 : A number of well known British helmsmen are members.

Address
The Clubhouse, Ashford Road, Ashford, Middlesex, TW15 1UA, England.
✆ 0784 243219
Secretary: 17 Plover Close, Moormede Park, Staines, Middlesex TW18 4RW
✆ 0784 461022

No-nonsense dinghy sailing for London residents at Queen Mary reservoir.

The R. Southampton YC clubhouse in Ocean Village marina in the port of Southampton.

Royal Southampton Yacht Club

This is another example of an old established club which behaves as if it has just discovered sailing and is bristling with new ideas for cruising, racing and shore activities. Southampton is a container port half way along England's south coast and 100 miles from London by road. Any fame still probably derives from the relatively brief period in the first half of this century when the port was the terminal for the big transatlantic liners, such as the *Normandie*, *Queen Mary* and *United States*. These brought with them industrialization which had its effect on the use of the immediate waters for yachts. Southampton has always had major yacht yards and remains the geographical centre for a very large yachting industry with hundreds of firms catering for every aspect of sailing and motor boating within a small radius.

Clubhouse
The clubhouse is exceptional having been built in 1988 to the requirements of the members and being part of a new development. It is within the city of Southampton and in sight of docks occupied by big ships. The marina, of which it is a part, is known as Ocean Village and was converted from old docks in the port. The club is built out over the water on two stories. It has a modern lobby with reception desk, restaurant, bar overlooking the marina with balcony, committee rooms and a functions room. There are some cabins for members and residential apartments.

A carved chair presented by the builder of the original clubhouse is in the lobby, the timber came from the 1884 demolition of the guild hall of the city, originally constructed in the 13th century.

There is a second clubhouse on the Beaulieu River about ten miles to the west in very rural surroundings; this small summer station was built in 1964, when the club had no other waterside premises. It is open four days a week in the summer and is a peaceful unspoilt spot with river moorings close by.

Waterside
The immediate (Ocean Village) marina has 400 berths and 12 visitor berths owned by the club. Leaving this, a yacht is in Southampton Water, a relatively narrow channel used by commercial shipping, but possible for racing by small yachts. Less than an hour's sail leads into the Solent for cruising, racing, anchoring, visits to harbours and other yacht facilities.

History
In the 19th century, yachts lay at moorings off the city of Southampton and also raced in Southampton Water. The Royal Southern Yacht Club, founded in 1837, had an imposing clubhouse (which still stands) looking out across this scene. This club did not meet the needs of all those resident in and near Southampton and the new club came into being in 1875 as Southampton Yacht Club. It took large premises in the main street of the city which actually led directly to the waterfront. Just two years later the royal warrant arrived with the title 'royal' and the privilege of a blue ensign defaced by the Southampton city shield and a crown on the union jack. The burgee today has the city device and crown, but the ensign

has been changed to an undefaced blue ensign, but with a crown in the middle of the union flag, which is unusual.

The street in which the club lay was heavily bombed in 1940, but it remained until 1957, when a move was made to a more residential area two miles inland. While the club continued to organize all kinds of sailing, the clubhouse was bound to be more of a weekday luncheon place and winter meeting place. It was large and used for innumerable meetings of yachting organizations without permanent headquarters. This second clubhouse was disposed of in 1987, when the land was redeveloped. At the same time the docks and waterfront of the city were being revived: old warehouses and sheds were pulled down and new bright housing was built. The club obtained a 999-year lease on the new premises. HRH The Prince Michael of Kent laid the foundation stone in 1987 and one year later opened the present clubhouse.

From its earliest days the club was active. The small boats sailed in Southampton Water, but the large yachts needed to be in the main part of the Solent and the Royal Southampton soon had a regatta day close to Cowes Week. For instance in 1897, the club is reported as having five small yacht regattas during the season, while its regatta for large yachts was on the Monday after Cowes Week (other non-Cowes clubs followed). Then was sailed the race for the Queen's Cup. This impressive gold trophy presented by Queen Victoria, for her diamond jubilee in 1897, remains the club's most important cup and is in a show case in the building. When Cowes Week extended to begin on the 'preceding' Saturday, the Royal Southampton took over that day, which is still gives. The Queen's Cup remains the principal trophy for that day (the exact class which is eligible has obviously varied over the years).

Classes
Cruiser-racer, offshore racer (CHS and local handicap); 420 and Optimist for juniors at Beaulieu.

Events and regattas
As already mentioned, the Royal Southampton traditionally runs the first day of Cowes Week every year and this includes a race for the Queen's Cup. It has one day in the Solent points series each season (Clarkson Cup). Since 1983, it has run a two-handed round the island (Wight), which has about 250 starters. Also now a series of four two-handed races: popularity possible because of owner crew problems. Spring and autumn Sunday morning series in Southampton Water revived and harks back to the 19th century. Two or three commercial sponsors support specific race programmes. Several cruising rallies under sail each season, some in France; dinghy weekends especially for juniors at Ginn's Farm station. Motor cruiser rallies. Charity pursuit race in December. Whitbread Round The World Race competitors dock by the club at initial start and last finish.

Winter lectures with suppers; new members cocktail party;

Members
990 : Admiral: HRH The Prince Michael of Kent

Address
1 Channel Way, Ocean Village, Southampton, SO1 1XE, England.
© 0703 223352

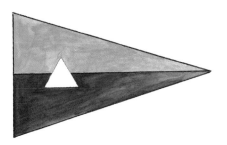

Little Ship Club

This club has a name not quite like any other. Founded in 1926, there was emphasis on the 'slow' motor cruisers of the day and 'serious' cruising and seamanship with them. If the image was one of the converted lifeboat, then that was because a secretary and enthusiast of the club owned one for many years. This was a Lt-Cmdr J.J.Quill RNVR, a character, who was a major player in the club's influence. Along with this theme went training during the week in the convenient clubhouse (see below) and a location essentially convenient for those who worked in 'The City' (London's financial district).

Clubhouse

The clubhouse, like that of the Royal Thames YC, is constricted by London's property market by taking the ground and first floor in a business block with offices above. Once one has entered the club, these are simply not noticeable. The site is on the embankment of the River Thames alongside Southwark bridge along a short approach known as Bell Wharf Lane, another name of ancient origin. This clubhouse was ready in June 1991, when the club moved in there. As in the past, the rooms are arranged not only for social occasions with a seventy seat dining room and clubroom and bar overlooking the Thames with balcony, but library and training accommodation. If the double doors are opened between clubroom and dining room, there is a capacity of 120 for special functions. There is sleeping accommodation of five two-berth cabins, lined in mahogany with brass portholes on to the river, available from Monday to Thursday. There is a chart room used for consulting charts, cruising directions, reading and writing. This is not a weekend clubhouse, but a purpose built town yacht club reflecting the ideas of the 1990s.

Waterside

Owing to restrictions imposed by the London River authorities, there are no alongside facilities. There is berthing in the London River in certain docks and basins within an easy taxi ride. However the members expect to keep their boats anywhere around the British coast and overseas, using the club to meet during the working week and in the winter.

History

The club was founded as a no-frills sailing and motor boating club with headquarters right in the financial district of London, enabling members to meet all through the working week. The first president was Claud Worth, then the doyen of cruising sailors in England. The activities consisted of rallies in the season and during the winter there were lectures and training of a notably high standard; this was long before the advent of national training schemes in Britain.

During World War II the club kept open in London. Because of defence restrictions on sailing and movement even on land around the coast, the London and Thames clubs actually prospered (see London Corinthian SC, page 37), since yachtsmen gathered to talk about their interest, sailed on inland waters and planned for post-war sailing. For many years over this period, the premises were at Beaver Hall on Garlick Hill, near the official residence of the Lord Mayor of London. This intensely central position

Second rebuild since the 1960s, in the City of London (financial quarter),
with a River Thames frontage.

played a big part in the unique nature of the club.

At a meeting soon after the war, the members were told that membership had actually expanded to 2,000 during the war, that the president was absent sailing German service yachts (see British Kiel YC) back to England, that a further membership figures consisted of members serving in the forces who paid no subscription and that the quarterly club journal was about to be reissued!

With the rebuilding of the City of London after World War II, the club moved into its own newly built block a short distance from Garlick Hill, but overlooking the Thames. This was along Bell Wharf, beside Southwark bridge. There were a number of floors and, for instance, a spacious lecture theatre. This served the members well during the 60s and 70s; then the roaring property values took over and the relatively new building was torn down to make room for offices which paid high rents. However the club was reserved the two bottom floors. During the period of building, members were able to use the Naval Club in the 'West End'. This exile ended in 1991.

Classes
The club is for cruising people. There are no racing classes.

Events and regattas
There are twenty annual cruising rallies in Britain and Europe and twenty-five annual cruising awards. The social programme at the clubhouse and at coastal rallies is extensive. Systematic training in accordance with schemes of the national authority.

Members
1,500

Address
Bell Wharf Lane, Upper Thames Street, London, EC4R 3TB, England.
℄ 071 236 7729

Part 2
A Certain Tradition

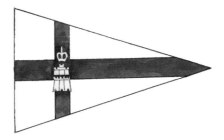

Royal Gibraltar Yacht Club

This is one of the very oldest yacht clubs in the world (see below) and has been 'royal' since 1933. Gibraltar is an immense cross roads of the sea for cruising yachts heading to and from northern Europe, with its vast numbers of yachts, and the cruising and racing waters of the Mediterranean and the Caribbean. It is also on the frequented Mediterranean-Caribbean route. However the club, while welcoming crews of visiting yachts, members of recognized yacht clubs and its own members' guests, continues with its own racing and social programme every season for sailing people living in Gibraltar. British servicemen and women stationed in Gibraltar have traditionally been an important part of the membership, though the numbers have now decreased considerably.

Clubhouse
This overlooks the harbour and has dinghy launching and alongside berthing for members only.

History
The Gibraltar Yacht Club was founded in June 1829 by Army officers of regiments stationed in the garrison. Very few clubs indeed had been formed before this date (see page 15) and then only in the British Isles. The club says that a minute from 1860 by the Governor of the colony states the club is the second oldest in existence, but the commodore of 1929, whose research is still published in the club rules, believed it was the eighth in the world after the Cork, Thames, Squadron,

Dee, Loch Long, Northern and Western. It at first was permitted to wear the White Ensign, but in 1842 in common with several clubs this was withdrawn in favour of the defaced Blue Ensign.

Classes
Offshore racer, cruiser-racer, Laser, Victory

Events and regattas
There is class racing on Wednesdays, Saturdays and Sundays throughout the season, May to October, and an annual regatta week for the Laser and Victory. The Victory (21ft, 6.3m) is the same as that based in Portsmouth, England, unusual in being discarded in 1934 by the Bembridge (Isle of Wight) SC and then adopted by an association in Portsmouth, which has since built 70 of these wooden keel-boats, including those shipped to Gibraltar. It is a class that on such a basis will continue as far as can be seen.

A race from Marbella for cruiser-racers is followed by a short inshore and there are usually two or three other offshore events. There have been occasional long ocean races from England finishing at Gibraltar. The Europa 92 finished there in May 1992.

Members
450 : Patron: HM The Queen.
Admiral: HRH Prince Philip.

Address
Queensway, Gibraltar.

Gibraltar, home of the oldest club outside the British Isles, now with modern marinas.

The famous facade of the New York Yacht Club in Manhattan.

New York Yacht Club

Superlatives are in order for describing the New York Yacht Club situated in the city of the world's richest men, being one of the most palatial clubs (what other is on six floors?), with a history second to none and the holder until 1983 of yacht racing's supreme prize: The *America*'s Cup. In the decade or so since then, the club has learned to live without The Cup, mounted as it was in a special room – or shrine. The room has disappeared, altered out of recognition during internal rebuilding. Some members, while in no way celebrating its loss, have said, that the change released new energy into the NYYC, promoting wider sailing activities, whereas before the cup was (almost) all.

Like the Royal Yacht Squadron (page 63), it historically resisted submitting its racing and rating rules to any national authority and it was not until 1942 that it at last joined the then North American Yacht Racing Union.

Clubhouse

The famous clubhouse is at 37 West 44th Street in down-town Manhattan, just off Fifth Avenue. In 1901 the club moved from its old premises at 67 Madison Avenue and has been there ever since. It was large and wealthy then, constructed on land donated by the billionaire commodore, J.P.Morgan, and still is. No other club extends to six floors, though the old building is surrounded by skyscrapers and modern blocks. The striking exterior is dominated by three decorative bay windows based on those found on the sterns of 17th century Dutch vessels. Actually the club was designed by the leading architect of the period in a style known as eclectic.

In this state preserved heritage building is the amazing model room. There is nothing like it in the world, with its forty-five ton stone fireplace, the walls covered in the half-models of 150 years of yachting and the extra big models of *America*'s Cup challengers and defenders in additional glass cases in the centre of the room (more of a hall or even a temple). Leading off the huge lobby are the grill room (like the 'tween decks of a sailing ship), members' rooms and on the first floor is one of the finest yachting libraries in the world, with a permanent librarian in charge. The dining room is of very high restaurant standard. There is a considerable amount of accommodation on the upper floors for members and their guests to stay, as befits a city club used mainly during the week.

In 1987 negotiations were begun to add a 'country clubhouse' at Newport, Rhode Island. This large house which became available following the death of a member is Harbour Court and has added a new dimension to the club in the sailing season.

History

On 30th July 1844, nine men met in the cabin of John Cox Stevens' yacht *Gimcrack* of 51ft (15.5m), moored off the Battery in New York Harbor. They decided to form the New York Yacht Club and Stevens was elected commodore. The first object was to hold a club cruise from New York to Newport, Rhode Island. Next month eight yachts did just that. In 1845 there was a race. This was through the Narrows, around a buoy in the Lower Bay and back. A time allowance system was instituted at 45 seconds per mile for each ton under the US Custom House Tonnage formula. In 1850 a letter was received by a member of the club, George Schuyler, from England. It was an invitation to send over one of the famed fast sailing New York pilot schooners as part of the world's first international exhibition to be held in England the next summer.

Stevens and some members decided to build instead, a yacht, based on – but an improvement of, the pilot schooners and take her to England to challenge the smartest yachts and yachtsmen in the world. She was named *America* and what happened we all know. In the event the club held and successfully defended the *America*'s Cup from 1851 to 1983. American yachts have won ninety-one out of the 104 races sailed and have retained the cup twenty-eight out of twenty-nine times. In its time it became a symbol of yachting supremacy. This supremacy was that of the defending club, the New York Yacht Club and the club surely represented the United States of America.

From 1845, the NYYC had a clubhouse at Elysian Field, now Hoboken, New Jersey, on the Hudson River. Races were started here and went out through the Narrows. This little clubhouse, a kind of pavilion, was preserved and moved several times and still exists today as an exhibit in Mystic Seaport, Connecticut. In 1859 a member and his yacht were expelled from the club for shipping a cargo of one hundred slaves from Africa to the southern USA. The same year the rating rule for the club was completely changed from sail area to length times beam, a matter which aroused considerably greater discussion. In 1859, a new site was found for a clubhouse at Staten Island owing to commercial congestion in New York. There was a further move in 1872 to a town house in Madison Avenue at 27th Street; in 1884 the club leased a three storey building at 67 Madison Avenue. There were also various summer stations started and then closed down over the years. In 1893 there were 1,000 members and the annual dues were $25. In 1894 the widow of a former member, and yacht owner, applied for membership. The committee decided that a woman could indeed be elected, but this was turned down by the general membership.

In 1912 members of the Royal Yacht Squadron purchased from a public house (the Eagle Hotel) in Ryde, Isle of Wight, the eagle and ornamentation from the schooner *America*, which had found its way there many years before as a door decoration. The NYYC had known about this, but despite efforts had been unable to purchase it. The Duke of Sutherland travelled to New York with the decoration and presented it as a gift from the RYS at a dinner in the clubhouse: it is still there.

All through these decades the history of the *America*'s Cup was essentially entwined with that of the NYYC. As a contest loomed so the club energies and programmes were devoted to it and as the year of the challenge arrived so also the social round fitted in. It must be remembered that the cup races were in the waters of New York. It was not until the 1930 defence that they were moved to Newport, RI; that was also the first time the J-class (the Universal Rule) was used, as it was in 1934 and 1937 only.

In the 20s and 30s, the new sport of ocean racing was welcomed by many club members. The primary race in the eastern USA was the Newport to Bermuda Race; though it was run by the Cruising Club of America, many of the leading members of the latter were also members of the NYYC. Inshore the leading sailors adopted the (European) International Rule, sailing 8-metre and 6-metre keel-boats rather than the equivalent American Universal Rule (which it was agreed to use for the bigger yachts).

In 1934 the club nearly lost the *America*'s Cup, when T.O.M. Sopwith's RYS challenger *Endeavour* won the first two races against Harold Vanderbilt's *Rainbow*. In the third race the British boat ran into a windless patch and was beaten. In the fourth race there was a celebrated protest case by Sopwith, the cause of much uninformed press comment. It must be remembered that the rules were those of the NYYC: neither national nor international rulings came into it. The NYYC called for a protest flag to be hoisted as soon as possible after the incident, but the British rules had always merely required a flag to be shown to the sailing committee 'at the first opportunity'. Amazingly Sopwith asked the opinion of his American observer on board, who was vague on the matter and subsequently the race committee of the NYYC (no international juries in those days) refused to hear the protest as the flag had not been hoisted early. *Rainbow* won the series 4–2.

The library at the Newport clubhouse, Harbour Court.

As mentioned, the club resolved to join NAYRU in 1942; then in 1945 it at last joined the Yacht Racing Association of Long Island Sound. In 1946 the club decided to use the CCA rule for its cruiser races. This is the modern way, but the power and single-mindedness of the old clubs (the Eastern YC near Boston was even slower to co-operate) was remarkable.

For years there had been a King's Cup when each king of England since Edward VII presented a trophy, the previous trophy being 'retired' after the death of the respective monarch. In 1953 Queen Elizabeth presented a Queen's Cup with a London hallmark dated 1775. The cup is used each year for a major race.The centenary of the club fell in the war years and was celebrated quietly, but the club was due to run a number of events and day regattas for the 150th year in 1994, some of them in conjunction with the most senior foreign clubs.

America's Cup today.
The only way for the NYYC to regain the *America*'s Cup is for the San Diego YC (page 88) to lose it to a foreign club and then several years later for the NYYC to win a challenge round and subsequently win abroad in a club designated yacht – rather like 1851 all over again.

Classes
Cruiser-racer, offshore racer (IMS, PHRF NYYC Cruising rules), 12-metres.

Events and regattas
There are a number of important trophies raced for every year; conditions and races vary from time to time as classes and racing tendencies change. As well as the Queen's Cup, there is the Corsair Cup, Astor Cups, US Navy Cup, Cygnet Cup, Nathanael Greene Herreshoff Medal, Brenton Reef Challenge Cup, NYYC Race Committee Trophy and others.

The NYYC Cruise is a series of races and social stopovers held annually in July, usually between Long Island Sound and Newport.

There are numerous social functions in the Manhattan and Newport clubhouses.

Members
2,500.

Address
37 West 44th Street, New York, NY 10036, USA. Harbour Court, 5 Halidon Drive, Newport, R.I.
℡ 0101 516 673 5781/0101 401 846 1000

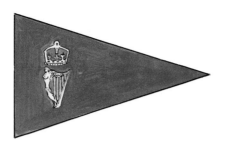

Royal Cork Yacht Club

This yacht club, at the village of Crosshaven within Cork harbour on the south coast of Ireland, has long been acknowledged as the oldest yacht club in the world with records dating from 1720. On page 15 there is a discussion about claims to this title. Partly because of this strong tradition, partly because of the superb waters in which it lies and partly because of the ever active Irish yachting scene, the club retains a strong programme and the membership of many yacht owners, cruising and racing.

Clubhouse

The present clubhouse is a modest single storey building, on the main road through the village, but fronting its own marina berthing on an estuary bank, or more exactly, the Owenboy River. As befits an Irish club there is a large bar, where the wines of the country might be considered as Murphy's stout and whiskey with an 'e'. There is also a dining room, club offices, storage and changing rooms. Races can be started from the club, but events for larger boats or high numbers would be by committee boat in the main harbour. The city of Cork itself is not accessible to yachts, being at the head of a creek, but about twelve miles by road. The town of Cobh, naval base and steamer terminal, more directly faces the waters of the harbour on the north side.

Waterside

Apart from the marina at the club, there is a second one within walking distance downstream at the Crosshaven Boatyard. This busy yard has also constructed many medium sized or large yachts in its time,

some famous. There are many moorings in the river, which is navigable at least one and a half miles above the club station. All kinds of sailing and racing can take place within the expanse of the harbour, without going into the Atlantic Ocean. However seaman have long known that Cork harbour is one of the world's most accessible ports in all weather.

History

Because of the natural qualities of the harbour and its indentation of the hinterland, travelling by boat there was often more convenient than a carriage or cart on a bumpy track in the 17th century. The more prosperous citizens had fast, smart and decorative sailing vessels for this purpose. So the famous paintings of the Water Club of Cork remain and date back to 1720, the club's claimed date of foundation, as shown on its crest.

The paintings show the club members sailing bluff bowed, gaff rigged cutters about 40ft (12m) long, of a type then used by pilots and revenue officers (who always needed fast sailers). The yachts engaged in manoeuvres under the command of an 'admiral', who used signal guns and flags. There were rules in force, indeed twenty-five of them, of which, for instance, number ten said, 'No boat presume to sail ahead of the admiral, or depart the fleet without his order, but may carry what sail she pleases to keep company'. The Lords of the Admiralty in London apparently granted the club its own ensign in 1759. The club headquarters were at Haulbowline Island, which is within the harbour. Here were held formal dinners: Rule

14 said *'Resolved, that such members of the club, or others, as shall talk of sailing after dinner be fined a bumper'*. Records become sparse towards the close of the 18th century, but a painting of Cork harbour in the national gallery in Dublin shows clearly the boats of the Water Club.

In 1806 the Marquess of Thomond and Lord Kinsale tried to revive the club, but ways had changed in the wars and activities were directed to competition among the sailing and rowing boats in the harbour. These races were combined with those of a recently formed Little Monkstown Club. In 1828, the remaining members of the old Water Club joined with this club to form the Cork Yacht Club. In 1830 it was granted the royal warrant, the third club in the world to be made so. At the same time 'founded 1720' was shown on all documents to leave no doubt of the ancestry. By 1845, there were 130 members and forty yachts. The annual subscription was then two pounds, the clubhouse was a small three storey building on the front street of Cobh and there was still an admiral (and vice admiral) as in the old days (though all other clubs had a commodore). Among appointments were a marine painter, nautical instrument maker and a flag maker: the latter was truly called Mrs Notter of Merchant's Quay, Cork.

In July 1860, at fairly short notice fifteen yachts from Dublin and the Royal Cork YC, of between 25 and 140 tons, raced from Dublin to Cork. The race was again sailed in 1861, 1862 and 1888. An east to west transatlantic race started from Cork in 1870 and was the finish of the west to east race in 1887.

In 1870 was formed the Munster YC (Royal Munster in 1872), which after forming at Monkstown moved to Crosshaven, while the Royal Cork stayed at Cobh, a place increasingly unsuitable for sailing. Many active sailors were members of both clubs and in 1968, they combined under the Royal Cork name. In 1969 and 1970, for the 250th anniversary, the club held a whole series of regattas, including class championships, cruising rallies and a race from the USA ending at the club. Currently the other clubs in the harbour are Cove (Cobh) Sailing Club, East Ferry YC and Monkstown Bay SC.

Classes
Cruiser-racer handicap using CHS, IMS and ECHO (an Irish national system); dinghies, National 18ft class, International Mirror, International Laser, Laser 2. Cork Harbour One-design (in the course of formation, 1993).

Events and regattas
In most years the club is host to an international or other major class championship; Half Ton Cup 1976, One Ton Cup 1981. Annual August 'at home' (replaces regatta), annual laying up supper with concert performance by each boat crew. Every even year since 1990, Cork Week (or using sponsor name, such as 'Ford Week') with huge offshore and cruiser-racer numbers from Britain and continent. Stopover port for R Western YC (page 19) Round Britain and Ireland Race and other round British Isles races, starting in England. October League (established for twenty years). Junior programme each season.

Members
1,100 : Flag officers are admiral, vice-admiral, rear-admiral, commodore. Yachts can carry an Irish blue ensign with tricolour of Ireland in corner and club crest in fly. British members can still claim Admiralty warrant for defaced blue ensign. Because of the unique antiquity of the club, there are many overseas members.

Address
Crosshaven, Co. Cork, Eire.
© 353 21 831023

The modern Royal Cork clubhouse with the alongside berthing of an ancient society, at Crosshaven.

The impressive frontage of the Royal Canadian Yacht Club summer station.

Royal Canadian Yacht Club

There are a few clubs in the world that assert an undoubted seniority by having the name of the nation as the sole name. Examples are the Yacht Club de France, Yacht Club Italiano and the Royal New Zealand Yacht Squadron. One of this exclusive band is the Royal Canadian Yacht Club with its two fine clubhouses, one in the city of Toronto and one on Toronto Island in Lake Ontario. Its history is close to that of all Canadian yachting, while its location in one of the great cities of North America, means that there is an energetic and resourceful membership, now and in the future. For many years some of its international fame rested on one of the great yacht racing challenges: the *Canada*'s Cup, sailed as a match race against the USA. The club was twice the challenger for the *America*'s Cup (1876 and 1881). Now the sailing and racing activities embrace a wide spectrum of yachting involving a vast number of members.

Clubhouse

The main clubhouse is open from May to September on Toronto Island, in effect a string of islands, with some sheltered inlets. With its long two-storeyed frontage of pillared balconies, it is an impressive headquarters. It was ópened on 10th June 1922, the foundation stone having been laid by HRH The Prince of Wales in 1919 on an extensive visit to the club. The club can be reached from downtown Toronto by ferry in ten minutes. In 1974 the yacht club merged with the Carlton Club, which resulted in the acquisition of a town clubhouse at 141 St George Street: this second clubhouse is retained for all year round use and is minutes away from the financial district.

In the main clubhouse there is a dining room, Ovens room (snack bar), Sailors' bar, as well as the usual offices and changing rooms. There are tennis courts and a swimming pool. The club rules are among the most extensive found anywhere, the rules for dress being particularly specific. 'Proper attire', as defined with club jacket, tie and trousers or Bermuda shorts with hose are required in the clubhouse with a few excepted areas. Ladies need equivalent and also children over nine years.

In 1993 the clubhouses were host to the annual meeting of the International Yacht Racing Union (IYRU), one of the very few occasions when the conference was other than in London.

Waterside

A marina and moorings adjoin the club area which also has boatyard services, fuelling point and yacht chandlery. Lake Ontario is about 165 nautical miles long, so the sailing is on fresh yet open water.

History

A very small group of persons were said to have met in 1850, though it was March 1852, when the Toronto Boat Club was formed. The object was for the members' yachts to meet every Saturday afternoon in the season, draw lots for a leader, who would head the fleet to garrison Wharf and back, after which the yachts dispersed. Like the Royal Yacht Squadron and other British clubs of the time, some of the activities were considered as training for the navy in time of war, or for experiments in naval architecture and ship handling for defence. (There had been naval engagements between Canada and the USA on the Great Lakes, barely forty years earlier.) When the title 'royal' was granted, the name of the club somehow changed to 'Canadian'. The present full name was assumed, though the records fail to show quite how!

Like many early clubs, the members at first used a small existing house in the city (near what is now Union Station); then it moved to a one storey building erected over a barge from where races were started, but this sank in 1858. After experiences with another floating clubhouse, the club eventually in 1868 built a spacious premises on a wharf at Simcoe street with verandahs and an observation platform. Industrialization caused the sale of this club in 1880 and the purchase of land on the Island. Meanwhile various sites in the city were used from time to time as town houses. A fine Edwardian clubhouse was built on the Island, but this was totally burnt in 1904. The club was rebuilt, but again lost by fire in 1918. The present clubhouse followed.

In 1860 The Prince of Wales (later Edward VII) visited the club for which a major regatta was organized, royal visits being a rare event in those days. In 1901 the Duke of York, (later George V) visited. In 1959, when the Queen and Prince Philip visited Toronto, the officers of the royal yacht *Britannia* were entertained by the club.

The *Canada*'s Cup originated when the yacht *Canada*, owned by AEmilius Jarvis of the R Canadian YC, beat a challenge by Charles Berriman of the Lincoln Park Yacht Club of Chicago in his yacht *Vencedor* (57ft, 17.4m) designed by William Fife of Scotland. Twelve challenges followed between the club and several American clubs until 1975, after which other Canadian clubs (eg Royal Hamilton YC) took part in the defence. Wins and losses have been roughly equally divided (unlike the *America*'s Cup) between the two nations over the years. No other countries are involved. Today single challenges are seldom popular and practicable for class, rating and sponsorship reasons. AEmilius Jarvis was commodore of the club on three separate occasions (two or three year terms, short as customary in North America). Born in 1860, he was a major owner and club member all his life. He died in 1940.

The two challenges for the *America*'s Cup under the name of the club in 1876 and 1881 were heavily defeated by the American defenders. The rules of the time gave rise to very unequal boats and after events the rules were changed confining the challenging club to one situated on salt water.

The sailing Olympics were held on Lake Ontario in 1976, but these were from a special harbour complex at Kingston at the other end of the lake. There were six classes, it was the only recent Olympics not to include the Star class and security was notably oppressive. The club has always played a major part in supplying sailors and helping organize the Canadian Olympic team. It has frequently represented Canada in the historic International 14ft Dinghy class (against Australia, United Kingdom and USA and occasionally others).

There is a strong junior programme, founded in 1925 with sixty boys; girls were admitted in 1956

Classes
At this club many classes are raced, including Cruiser-Racer (IMS, IOR and PHRF); Albacore, C&C 27; C&C 34; 8-metre; International Dragon; Etchells 22; International 14; J24; Laser and variants; Shark.

Events and regattas
Typical major regattas in one year were: Open Regatta, Easter Seals Yellow Pages (Charity) races, Mid-summer level regatta, International 14 footer Worlds, IYRU World Team racing with numerous races and prizes for each class. Cruising sailors and power fleet meetings.

Members
3,000 plus 800 associate members. There is a commodore (two year term) and six vice commodores (three years); no rear commodore. Qualifications for flag officers are stringent including yacht ownership, period as a member and others. Patron: HRH Prince Philip. There are fourteen categories of member of the club.

Address
141 St George Street, Toronto, Ontario, M5R 2L8, Canada.
✆ 0101 416 967 7245

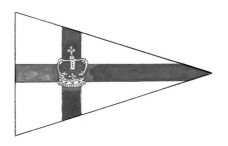

Royal Yacht Squadron

The term 'yacht club' was invented here, but a king later gave the club the name of the 'squadron' and others became clubs. Some say this is the world's most exclusive gentlemen's club (ladies cannot be members), the number being limited to 450. These gentlemen are mainly from the aristocracy, titled persons, landowners, officers of the household division (the Guards), other good regiments and the Navy, plus an element of one-time flag officers of the Royal Ocean Racing Club. A number are members of one or more London clubs (White's, Brooke's and so on). New members are still elected by ballot and blackballing is possible. There is a very high percentage of yacht ownership.

Today the magnificent location of the Royal Yacht Squadron castle at Cowes means it remains a centre for first class yacht racing: some of the most important regattas and races in England are based here or use its starting line. The line and its modern facilities are frequently loaned to other clubs; for instance the Island Sailing Club for the Round the Island Race (about 2,000 starters) and the RORC for the Fastnet Race (about 250 starters).

Clubhouse

This is in a castle built as a fort by King Henry VIII in 1539. It was in military occupation for three centuries, but the guns were never fired in anger. In the 19th century it became a residence for the governor of the Isle of Wight. He vacated it in 1857 and the RYS negotiated a lease from the Crown, in due course hoisting its flag there on 6th July 1858: a general meeting of members was held there four days later. The only previous clubhouse had been in a modest building, a few yards beyond the castle gate from 1825 until the move.

The ground floor consists of the members' dining room, ladies' dining room, morning room, ladies drawing room and a conservatory-balcony as well as offices, changing rooms and kitchens. In addition there is the conspicuous 'platform' with the battlements in front. These are the features immediately visible to yachtsmen sailing off the castle in the vicinity of the start line. From here races are controlled with the flag signals and electrically operated cannon immediately below.

On the first floor are bedrooms and the library. Throughout all these rooms and corridors are historic paintings, trophies and mementoes. The lawn looks out over the west Solent; on a fine day when racing is in progress the view framed by the carefully tended flower beds is one of the sights of this world.

Waterside

Everything is historic where the Squadron is concerned: the stone jetty and steps outside its entrance gate are reserved for members and 'officers on Her Majesty's business'. Here where many kings, queens and princes have landed and embarked, members can be ferried out to yachts by launch. It is exposed in north and east winds. There are a couple of member buoys just offshore and piling reserved for members' yachts up river. Visitor berths do not arise, as the whole of Cowes harbour is adjoining.

History

As the long period of war drew to a close in

The Royal Yacht Squadron castle at dusk.

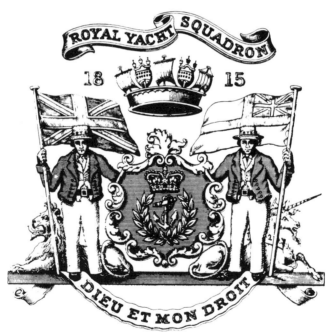

The elaborate seal of the RYS with jack tars, a naval crown, date of establishment and the motto of the monarchy itself.

1815, club life in London expanded, yet the two leading clubs in St James's, White's and Brooke's, were savage in their blackballing, partly the work of 'Beau' Brummel and the 'Dandies'. Gentlemen were in the process of forming new societies. In a town where this club or that club was envisaged, forty-two gentlemen, about half of them titled, met on 1st June 1815 at the Thatched House Tavern, St James's, London, and formed The Yacht

Club. This term had never before been known, despite several societies existing for regattas and rallies (page 15). Any yacht over 10 tons was registered and the members, at first, expected merely to meet at Cowes in the summer and have a dinner in a hotel and another meeting and dinner in London in the spring.

After the battle of Waterloo on 15th June 1815 and the arrival of years of peace and particularly for Britain, its years of relative prosperity, yachting activities expanded. On 17th September a special meeting was called at East Cowes during which the following letter was read out: 'Sir, The Prince Regent desires to be a member of The Yacht Club and you are to consider this as an official notification of His Royal Highness's desire. I have the honour to be, sir, Your obedient humble servant, Charles Paget'. The prince was immediately elected and the following spring two other royal princes joined. In 1820, the Prince Regent became king and the title was changed to the Royal Yacht Club.

On 10th August 1826, the club first gave a race for a gold cup, value £100, starting at 9.30 a.m. and on a course around the Solent. There was a ball that evening in East Cowes, followed by a dinner on Friday and a firework display in West Cowes after it. That was the beginning of Cowes Week, racing and Friday fireworks having been held (except for war years) ever since. In 1833 King William IV declared that the club was to become known as 'the Royal Yacht Squadron of which His Majesty is graciously pleased to consider himself the head'. The burgee was fixed as a red cross on white with a crown on the intersection and the ensign, as the White Ensign of the Royal Navy. As far as can be reckoned, there were by then six royal clubs for yachts in Britain, one in Gibraltar and one in Sweden (page 165).

Flags.

In Britain the use of the varying national maritime ensigns, red, white and blue was quite complex. The Navy used all three, merchant ships used the red and several yacht clubs used the white to show that their craft were not commercial, thus escaping port dues. One Irish club actually requested that its yachts might fly a green ensign. In 1842, the RYS asked the Admiralty if it could use the blue, because of confusion with other clubs using the white, which evidently was not specially prized. However the Admiralty decided instead to withdraw the white ensign from six clubs which currently used it and leave it with the RYS only. However the arrangement was botched and several more clubs were left after 1842 with the white.

For a number of years the matter was disputed and it became the subject of petitions and papers in the House of Commons. In 1863, the Royal Navy gave up the red and blue ensigns, all warships flying only the white, as they do today. This effectively ended the matter with only the RYS allowed to fly the white in addition to the Navy. Other clubs were granted various versions of the red and blue as recounted in these pages.

By 1834, the Squadron had 148 members owning 101 yachts totalling 10,000 tons register and these employed 1,200 seaman. In 1851, following the establishment of the New York Yacht Club, the schooner yacht *America*, owned by John Cox Stevens, commodore, and a syndicate, arrived in Cowes looking for racing. The story is well known and here will only be mentioned its aspects from that of the RYS. The commodore, the Earl of Wilton, had been welcoming, but for reasons that have never been clear, no matches were arranged for the would-be challenger. It may have been that owners were set in their routine, or perhaps, to some extent, in the hands of their professional skippers. Presumably the early August (Cowes Week) regatta did not provide a suitable class. Somehow the race of 22nd August for a One Hundred Guinea Cup of solid silver 'open to all nations' became scheduled and someone must have initiated the extraordinary idea of a race clockwise around the Isle of Wight.

The result we all know, but the RYS was closely involved in the protest which followed in that *America* and some other yachts had not rounded the Nab Light which was a float close to the eastern corner of the island. Since the notice of race and the sailing instructions were contradictory, the protests were withdrawn. It would have made no difference to the result. In the series of challenges from Britain which followed over the years, various clubs were concerned. The RYS came back in 1885 with Sir Richard Sutton's *Genesta* (beaten by *Puritan*); then in 1893 and 1895, when the brilliant but eccentric member, Lord Dunraven challenged with *Valkyrie II* and *III*. The acrimonious dispute which followed resulted in his expulsion from the NYYC. The remaining RYS challenges were by T.O.M.Sopwith in 1934 and 1937 and by an RYS syndicate with *Sceptre*, on which the members were badly advised, in 1958. The Cup returned on exhibition to Cowes for a few days during Cowes Week 1991.

The then Prince of Wales was elected commodore in 1882 and was at once pitched into a controversy over the newly formed Yacht Racing Association, one of whose main objects was to unify racing and rating rules throughout Britain. Since its foundation the RYS had used its own rules, as indeed did other clubs. The Prince was also president of the YRA and under his influence the dispute, which had damaged regatta entries for several years, was settled. From 1886 a new YRA rating rule brought the owners back into racing. Though it was to have its own problems in the future, these were no longer the concern of the RYS alone.

In the first half of the 20th century the emphasis was on the International classes (8-metre, 6-metre etc) and there were major races for cups such as the British-America Cup. *Britannia* and other yachts of the 'big class' which passed through various rating rules ending with the American J-class, were owned sometimes by members of the RYS and raced many days each season at Cowes, as well as touring the English and Scottish coasts. First Edward VIII, as Prince of Wales then King, raced *Britannia* followed by George V. She was scuttled on his death and her fittings were distributed among the many clubs at which she raced.

From 1949 HRH Prince Philip, Duke of Edinburgh, raced regularly in Cowes Week, often accompanied by several other members of the royal family. The royal yacht *Britannia* was usually moored in Cowes Roads for the first half of the Week. The Prince owned successively a Flying Fifteen, a Dragon and a large classic ocean racer *Bloodhound*. When the last of these had been sold he chartered a suitable racing boat for the Week.

The practice of each club in Cowes Week, which had grown to nine days of racing, giving its regatta, with different start lines and race instructions, continued until 1964. Then was formed the Cowes Combined Clubs resulting in uniform instructions and the use of the famous RYS line for all racing each day. From 1991, the racing reduced to eight days, as the last Sunday found little support and every other year the large Fastnet fleet left on the Saturday. The Squadron days remained, as ever, Tuesday, Wednesday and Thursday.

From 1953 the wife of a member was allowed to stay with her husband in the castle; in 1964 the ladies' dining room and changing room were allotted. Ladies may not however enter through the main door, nor are they permitted into a number of rooms, except when these are opened for a dance or particular function. From 1969, there were created Lady Associate Members.

Classes
International Dragon, International Etchells 22, Darings and on regatta days other keel-boat classes, races open to non-members. Cruiser-racer, offshore racer (CHS and IMS), race for RYS team in RORC and other series.

Events and regattas
Annual three days in Cowes Week, as described. This includes many trophies , the chief are *Britannia* Cup presented by King George VI and the New York YC Cup. June weekend regatta for all classes. Solent Points races (shared by clubs); regattas for various classes as arranged. Start of a number of RORC races each season. Reception for all Admiral's Cup crews on the lawn before each series. Club charter flotillas abroad. RYS ball on Monday of Cowes Week. Two general meetings per year in London and Cowes.

Members
Limited to 450. Patron: HM The Queen.
Admiral: HRH Prince Philip.
Hon member: HRH The Princess Royal.

Address
The Castle, Cowes, Isle of Wight, PO31 7QT, England.
✆ 0983 292191

Larchmont Yacht Club

Long Island Sound at 41° North, with New York city at its western end and the open Atlantic at the other is one of world's longest established and most frequented yachting waters. It is also very large, compared for instance with equivalent sheltered water in Australia and Europe, described in these pages. The Sound is 90 miles long and 20 miles wide at the centre, narrowing at the ends. Some 140 sailing and yacht clubs are located along its shores and on the other side of Long Island. They are grouped by US Sailing under the Yacht Racing Association of Long Island Sound, the Eastern Long Island Yachting Association and the Great South Bay YRA. One of the most distinguished of this huge number is the Larchmont Yacht Club. Larchmont is on the mainland, in New York state, near the far western end of the Sound, sheltered in Larchmont Harbor.

Clubhouse
The dignified clubhouse right on the waterfront was built as a private house in 1880 and acquired by the club in 1887. The club immediately added an east wing. Ten years later was added a west wing, which tripled the size of the original house. Since then there have been further additions and the result is an imposing frontage. The situation is not far from Interstate 1 and 95, a highway which runs up the whole east coast of the USA.

It goes without saying that there are large public rooms with a restaurant and other facilities of a standard second to none in the world and demanded by the yachtsmen resident in New York and its hinterland.

Waterside
There are moorings off the club within Larchmont Harbor and guest moorings. Dinghies can be launched at the club; there are three hoists for keel-boats and a small boatyard for members only. Sailing dinghies on 'floats'(pontoons). Fuel dock, but no alongside mooring, the nearest marinas being in adjacent harbours, two miles away or more.

Just to the east is the inlet of Mamaroneck, while directly south across the Sound, about six miles is the major sailing area of Manhasset Bay; south-east twelve miles are Oyster Bay and Cold Spring Harbor.

History
On Memorial Day (end of May) 1880, five young owners of small sandbaggers, sloops and catboats moored in Horseshoe Harbor, sitting round a camp fire after a day's racing, discussed the possibility of a yacht club. One month later, eighteen men met and formed themselves into the Larchmont YC. The first clubhouse was a Union church on the waterfront at a rent of $3 for three years, it could be used as a clubhouse, except on Sundays, when it was required for services! However in 1884, as the membership expanded, a lease was taken on a house on the western side of Larchmont Harbor, at an annual rent of $5,000. Then the present building and eleven acres were purchased in 1887, at a price of $100,000. In the light of currency values in those days, it seems that the members were already wealthy.

By 1910 there were 833 members and 288 yachts, of which 155 were power yachts. Sixteen schooners were listed; eleven of these were over 100 feet (30.5m).

Frostbite dinghies at the Larchmont Yacht Club.

The Corporate Seal of the Larchmont Yacht Club testifies to its old and continuous place in the sailing world.

Larchmont Race Week remains a famous fixture throughout the eastern US. At its peak it attracted up to 500 boats for daily racing in the third week of July. It was started in 1895. One result of the high standards which have always prevailed was a major settlement of the old Bermuda (rig) versus gaff of the early part of the century. In a series of ten races in 1917, the O-class one-designs with gaff rig, admitted a single Bermuda boat as a trial. The Bermuda rig won all but two of the races. Its impact on all new one-designs and other classes would surely not have been so wide if this had not happened at Larchmont.

In the 1930s a number of West Wight Scows were brought from England and regular winter dinghy racing began for the first time anywhere in the temperate part of the continent. The name 'frostbite racing' stuck and was exported to England and elsewhere. Over the many years the classes sailed at the club have varied with modern cruiser-racers since the 1920s and different one-design classes coming and going. Larchmont has typified the American dominance in keel-boats such as the International One-Design class, the 210, the Herreshoff S and the Luders 16, but there has been strong support for long established centreboard classes such as the Lightning, Thistle and Snipe. In the Race Week of 1954, there was a 12-metre class, a cruiser racer class and 22 other classes.

For a number of years there was official support in the club for other sports including golf, trap shooting, swimming, bowling, iceboating and poker.

Classes
Cruiser-racer up to maxi size (PHRF and IMS). International One-Design, International Etchells 22, Shields, Sonar, Herreshoff S. Frostbite dinghies in the winter.

Events and regattas
Larchmont Race Week in July now on two successive weekends for cruiser racers and keeled one-designs, mid-week for juniors. Annual distance race, May (over 38 of these so far sailed). Labor Day weekend regatta, Columbus Day weekend regatta. Some championships each year at North American or International level. Group cruises.

Dinner-dances at opening of Larchmont Race Week, New Year's Eve; 'cook-outs' on major summer holidays. Many other functions of all kinds. Other activities currently include swimming pool, tennis, ladies' bowling, men's bowling and bridge.

Members
Officially limited by rules to 600, but these are 'regular' with total of 1,200 in all categories. There are three flag officers and a Fleet Captain; there are twenty-six committees of various sorts. The regatta committee is the largest with thirty-one members; smallest is the year-book committee with two. A 1992 photograph of 'officers and trustees of the club' shows twelve blazered men and the chaplain.

Honorary members: the President of the United States, the Secretary of Defense, the President of US Sailing and the flag officers of the New York Yacht Club. Dues (subscriptions) in 1992 for regular member aged 32 or over was $6,000 for entry and $2,000 annually.

Address
Woodbine Avenue, Larchmont, NY 10538, USA.
✆ 0101 914 834 2440

The Fastnet Rock: immortal rounding-mark and reason for the existence of the RORC.

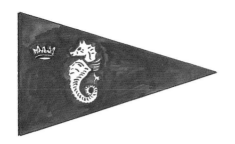

Royal Ocean Racing Club

The Royal Ocean Racing Club, London, is unique in that it is the only yacht club in the world, based in a full time clubhouse, that exists solely for the purpose of giving a programme of ocean races. With a clubhouse right in the most fashionable part of London, it runs every year a series of between seventeen and twenty-two events. These are predominantly around the coast of Britain, but are also overseas and are anything from 120 miles long to transocean(s) events. The membership is a mixture of many nationalities, although the British inevitably are in a big majority. To become a member it is necessary to have completed a Fastnet Race as an efficient member of a crew, or two alternative authorized races. In Britain the national authority for yachting, leaves all matters concerned with offshore racing in the hands of the RORC; in the clubhouse are offices for handling all aspects of ocean racing, while there are also the facilities of a London club. It therefore has at least three roles.

Clubhouse

This is at 20 St James's Place in the heart of London's club land and a very expensive residential quarter. On the ground floor are club and race offices with about fifteen full time staff. On the first floor is the bar, meeting place for ocean racing men from many parts of the world, a dining room and two other rooms which can be used for meetings, reading or writing. Nearby in St James's are such towering London 'gentlemen's clubs' as the Athenaeum, Brooke's, the Carlton and White's.

Above the oak door with its seahorse badge, flies the blue ensign defaced by a naval crown.

Waterside

The RORC has a further base in Cowes. This is in Prospect House, previously owned by the late Sir Max Aitken Bt. There are offices opening to the main street, a window for notices and accommodation for staff only. In the nature of its role, there are no permanent berths for members' yachts.

History

The club was formed when the crews of six yachts who had sailed in August 1925 in a new race from Ryde (in the Solent) around the Fastnet Rock off south-west Ireland and back to Plymouth, decided to have an Ocean Racing Club, the object of which was to hold at least one 600 mile race annually.

This race for seaworthy cruisers had arisen amid considerable controversy because Weston Martyr, a yachting writer, had taken part in the new New London to Bermuda races of 1923 and 1924. Organized by some members of the newly formed Cruising Club of America it was about 620 miles. Martyr and others pressed for an equivalent in British waters. It was hoped that the Royal Cruising Club would run it, but its committee considered the idea too risky and unseamanlike (rather as the Island Sailing Club, Cowes, turned down the single-handed transatlantic in 1960). It thus became logical to start a new club which approved of ocean racing in British waters. The word 'ocean' was used in the American sense where it means 'sea' and implied racing at sea, rather than in sheltered waters, the latter being the norm for first class yacht racing in Europe at the time.

As the membership grew, the club began to look for premises in London: a clubhouse was first opened at 2 Pall Mall in 1936. In November 1940, the club received a direct hit in an air raid, the steward was killed and the building destroyed. A short lease was then taken on 20 St James's Place and despite the fear that it would also be hit, it was opened as a club by King Haakon of Norway in July 1942. It became a place for hospitality to allied naval officers and plans for post-war ocean racing. Another World War II activity was the running of a design competition for an ocean racer of 32-35ft (9.75-10.67m)LWL for prisoners of war in Germany. It was won by an RAF Flight-Lieutenant in Oflag IVC.

Meanwhile before the war, the number of races and entries had risen each year. In 1930, there were four events (Fastnet, Channel, Santander, Dinard); in 1934, six; in 1937, eight; in 1938, ten. Other typical courses were Heligoland, La Baule, Ijmuiden, Southsea to Brixham, Southsea to Harwich. Within about five years of the first race, owners, particularly in the USA, began building yachts specially for ocean racing and also intended to fit the rating rule used by the club, simply called the RORC rule. American yachts won the Fastnet in 1928, 1931, 1933 and 1935. By the mid-30s, the 'ocean racer' distinct from the cruising yacht had arrived and the RORC with its rule and its courses had a major influence upon its development.

From the first post-war season of 1946, where a RORC entry was sent over to the Newport-Bermuda Race, through 1947 when the biennial Fastnet was revived and in the following years, ocean racing was the peak of yachting. The *America*'s Cup appeared to be finished (it actually started again in 1957 after a 20-year break) and the old keeled day-racers were few and far between. In the van of this new racing was the RORC with its challenging courses. These were sailed by amateurs and their friends and the boats seemed to be more and more able to handle all weather and finish races in conditions which some years before would have meant heaving-to or running for shelter. Other clubs ran shorter passage races for these boats, which then were used some weekends as inshore racers. When not actually racing they

made comfortable and very seaworthy fast cruising yachts.

The RORC rating rule for establishing corrected times (handicap order) and its safety rules became widely adopted everywhere in the world outside North and South America. In these places the equivalent systems of the Cruising Club of America and other US clubs such as the Storm Trysail Club and Midget Ocean Racing Club were used.

In 1929, the club applied for the royal prefix, but this was rejected by the Home Office. However it was granted in November 1931, when the club became the Royal Ocean Racing Club. Its emblem is simply a seahorse with the tail curled back, designed by being carved from wood by the first secretary, leading pioneer and winner of the Fastnet twice, Lt-Cmdr E.G.Martin. It is a special heraldic breed: *Hippocampus rorcus*. On the burgee is the white seahorse and naval crown; on the blue ensign granted to the RORC is simply a white naval crown. The club tie is quite famous and shows white seahorses on a dark blue field.

In 1957 four members of the RORC presented a trophy to be called the Admiral's Cup for a team race between three British ocean racers and the same number of visiting American yachts, the latter having been coming over for the Fastnet since the 20s. In the following Fastnet year, the club was asked to run the races and French and Dutch yachts took part. Thereafter the number of foreign teams participating increased each year until 1975 when nineteen teams were at Cowes. They raced not only in the Fastnet, but the Channel Race and two inshore races in Cowes Week to give total points. There were again nineteen teams in 1975 and 1979, but then the numbers fairly steadily decreased to eight in 1991 and 1993.

The type of inshore-offshore race was a new concept and in due course became copied around the world. Derivative events have been run by the Cruising Club of America (CCA), the Cruising Yacht Club of Australia (page 86) and the Cercle de la Voile de Paris, which initiated the One Ton (and Half Ton etc) Cup.

In the late 60s continental ocean racing men pressed for the rating rules of the CCA and the RORC to be combined, as they believed this would mean a number of

The Admiral's Cup,
first raced for in 1957.

advantages. The fusion was achieved in 1969 and the resulting International Offshore Rule (IOR) was used by the club from its 1971 season onwards. It also amalgamated its safety and equipment rules with those of the USA and in a tabular form which had also originated in America, grading races of varying severity. For nearly twenty years the IOR gave outstanding racing, but by about 1990, for a number of known reasons, it was declining in use in RORC races.

By 1991, except for the Admiral's Cup, it was no longer used and the club, in combination with UNCL in Paris had brought back a rating rule of its own, the Channel Handicap System (CHS). Like the previous rating rules run by the club, all the major events in Britain and also Ireland quickly came to use it. In 1993 the IOR was used for the last time in the Admiral's Cup.

If this history is rather longer than other clubs in this work, it is because few clubs, as such, have had such a profound and continuous influence on the way racing is conducted around the world and the design and equipment of sailing yachts of many kinds.

Classes

Offshore racer and cruiser-racer, using CHS and current safety and equipment rules. No size limit, but yachts are divided into classes by rating bands. Results additionally given in some races on IMS rating. Numbers of starters vary between 35 and 300 yachts.

The RORC runs a separate rating office with half a dozen staff. This rates competitors under all rules and rules for other events (e.g. one-designs and Whitbread racers). Its ratings are used by other clubs and organizations in a number of other countries to whom a service is given.

Events and regattas

Seasons follow a Fastnet and non-Fastnet alternate years. Programmes in the early 90s show more than twenty events each year. Starts occur in England, Scotland, Ireland, France, USA and Hong Kong and go the same countries plus Netherlands, Spain and the Philippines. There are some inshore races in conjunction with offshore to make a series or for early season tune up. Samples are Solent-Torquay, Harwich-Scheveningen, English Channel zig-zag courses, Hartlepool-Ijmuiden, Plymouth-Bayona, transatlantic, Round Ireland, Round Britain and Ireland, Burnham-Ostend, Dublin-Isle of Man-Dublin, Clyde-Brest.

The social programme consists of an informal prize-giving in the clubhouse in London one weekday evening after each race, an annual cocktail party on the lawn of the Royal Yacht Squadron and an annual dinner and prize-giving in London. There are a very large number of annual and race orientated trophies.

Members

3,500 : Each member must have qualified in the Fastnet or other races (see above). There is an Admiral and flag officers. Patron: HM The Queen. Life honorary members include the Kings of Norway, Greece, Spain and HRH Prince Philip, HRH Prince Charles and HRH Prince Bernhard of the Netherlands. Many naval attachés in London and officials in leading clubs are ex-officio honorary members.

Address

20 St James's Place, London, SW1A 1NN, England
✆ 071 493 2248
Rating office: Seahorse Building, Bath Road, Lymington, Hampshire, SO41 9SE, England.
✆ 0590 677030

20 St James's Place:
the priceless RORC clubhouse
in the 'West- end' of London.

The Royal Ulster's clubhouse and surroundings.

Royal Ulster Yacht Club

This is one of the old established clubs of the UK which has managed to retain its Victorian clubhouse and with the arrival of marina berthing has taken on a new aspect of active sailing. It is the senior club in the province of Ulster, in effect Northern Ireland. As well as being a senior social institution in the province, it also has a history which includes no less than five challenges for the *America*'s Cup.

Clubhouse

The club is at Bangor, a medium sized town on the south shore of Belfast Lough. This lough is actually a wide estuary in the approach to Belfast and there is immediate access to the open sea. The large Victorian building has changed little since it was opened to members on 15th April 1899. The club is open all the year round and has a busy dining room and bar. It is significant that a changing room and showers were not added until 1978.

Waterside

When Bangor marina was opened in 1990, there was at last secure mooring near the clubhouse for members' yachts. Strangely for one hundred years or so, there were never sheltered moorings near the clubhouse. (A number of large Victorian clubs in the UK were established in the same circumstances and have moved to smaller modern buildings by the water). The moorings in Belfast Loch actually suffered from boats being lost during gales year after year and whole classes moved to the more sheltered Strangford Lough, five miles south of Bangor or even to Dunloaghaire near Dublin. When a marina

was built at Carrickfergus on the north side of Belfast Lough, some boats moved there, a long way from the club by land. Bangor marina has changed all that and autumn racing in the mild climate can take place until December.

History

The club crest, since its foundation in 1866, has been the bloodthirsty 'red hand of Ulster' on a white shield under a crown and this appears on the Blue Ensign granted in 1869.

Earlier still in 1824, a few yacht owners formed the Northern Yacht Club. It held a regatta in Belfast in July 1925 and another on the Clyde in the same year. Two years later the Northern was split into Irish and Scottish clubs with a loose alliance between the two. In 1830 the Irish division was dissolved and its assets transferred to what is now the Royal Northern Yacht Club in Scotland.

Early regattas of the Royal Ulster YC followed the fashion of the day, with a few large yachts racing once a year in the lough, with shore side amusements, bands and rowing races. Some events in the UK still follow this form, but they tend to be 'town carnivals and regattas': racing sailors have long ago established their own fixtures. The first commodore was the Marquess of Dufferin and Ava, who was at times Governor-General of Canada, Ambassador to Russia and Viceroy of India; he had the title 'Vice-Admiral of Ulster'. Meetings were first held in the Athanaeum Rooms in Belfast. After renting two successive houses at Bangor, the present clubhouse site was acquired in 1897 and some more land round it in 1905.

Shamrock IV.
Sir Thomas Lipton
challenged through
the club in all his
America's Cup
forays, 1899-1930.

The annual regatta was one of those of the 'big boat' circuit in the early part of this century. As in a number of clubs, flags from the royal cutter *Britannia* were presented after she was scuttled. A number of one-designs were started over the years: Shakespeare class (1902), River class (1921), Dancing class (1924), Clipper class (1936) and Glen class (1947). The River and Glen still race on Strangford Lough. At one time there were ten Swallows, which now are only in Chichester harbour on the south coast of England.

Between 1898 and 1930, the five challenges to the New York Yacht Club by Sir Thomas Lipton for the *America*'s Cup, which had to be on behalf of a club, were made by the Royal Ulster Yacht Club. There is no record that the boats ever came to Northern Ireland. In 1970 the club presented the Sir Thomas Lipton Memorial Trophy for the yacht that has won the right to challenge (since unlike the earlier days, there are now multiple national challenges).

Classes
International Dragon, Waverley, Bay, Laser, Mirror, Topper, Enterprise, cruiser-racer (CHS).

Events and regattas
There are cruising musters, occasional tall ships visits, regular points races, offshore races to Scottish ports, a one-design keel-boat weekend and still the annual regatta. A strong fixture list runs from early April to late October.

Members
812 : Patron: HM The Queen. Commodore: HRH The Duke of Gloucester (and his father before him, son of King George V). In 1961, the Queen and Prince Philip visited the clubhouse and HRH Prince Edward did so in June 1991.

Address
101 Clifton Road, Bangor, County Down, BT20 5HY, Northern Ireland.
✆ 0247 270568

Koninklijke Nederlandsche Zeil-en Roeivereeniging

The club gives its name in English as the Royal Netherlands Yacht Club and it is the senior club in Holland. The full name also includes, as can be seen, rowing. As with most Dutch clubs, it is primarily an organization for running regattas and the main features of the clubhouse are for the immediate use of sailors, with storage, race office and bar. There are meeting in winter and other times, but these are not necessarily at the clubhouse.

Clubhouse
The present two-storey building at Muiden was built in 1953. It has a restaurant and bar together with the offices of the secretariat. It is used in both summer and winter, with the restaurant being used for lectures, bridge events and parties.

History
In the oldest traditions of yachting, the club began its life in Amsterdam, organizing sailing and rowing regattas under the eyes of spectators. Five years after it was founded in December 1847, King William III gave permission to use the title 'royal' and a warrant was issued for a special ensign. In 1890, the club co-founded the Royal Netherlands Yachting Association (now the national authority KNVWV) and in 1917 the national rowing equivalent. The RNYC remains 'honorary presiding club' of both authorities. In 1953, the club moved its base from Amsterdam to the ancient fortress town of Muiden, at the mouth of the Vecht river. This is far better situated for modern sailing and racing. Since 1977, there has been a second base at the yacht harbour of Buyshaven in Enkhuizen.

The privileged ensign remains as granted in 1852. On the white section of the Dutch tricolour is King William's crowned gold initial in a blue diamond. The same emblem is on the burgee.

Classes
Cruiser-racer, J24, Dragon

Events and regattas
There is a strong cruising element and cups for cruises and cruising logs. Out of season activities include lectures, bridge, happy hours and other social events. Regular sailing events are the Flevo Race, EC Laser Masters and in keeping with tradition, an international rowing regatta 'Kon. Holland Beker'. The club frequently runs major international fixtures such as the World Youth Sailing Championship in 1990 and the Dragon Gold Cup in 1993.

Members
950: President of Honour: HRH Prince Bernhard

Address
Postbus 30, 1398ZG, Muiden, Netherlands.
✆ 02942 1540

Muiden, club harbour of KNZR.

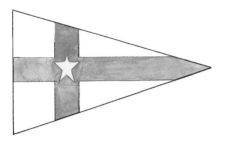

Starcross Yacht Club

This club, on the west bank of the estuary of the River Exe in south-west England, has a strong claim to be the oldest continuous yacht or sailing club in the world (page 15). It is the oldest in Britain. Its first known regatta was in August 1775, though it probably functioned before that. (The Royal Cork Yacht Club was dormant from 1763 to about 1803). Today it remains extremely active with a number of racing dinghy classes.

Clubhouse

This is on Powderham Point, in the estate of the Earl of Devon who is Patron of the club. The current building is a single story purpose built club opened in July 1966, with large club room from which racing can be watched and a kitchen and servery. Nearby, built slightly later, is an elevated starting box, for race officer control. An older building is used for changing rooms and storage; this previously was a clubhouse built in 1957. Before that the club simply operated from Starcross village, one mile south.

Waterside

Two slipways for launching racing dinghies lead directly from the club complex into deep water, except at an hour either side of low water spring tides. As low water springs is always around midday, one can go out in the morning and back in the afternoon, especially for a sail downstream. There is continuous effort and expenditure on maintaining the sea wall; the members pitch in to some of the work themselves. The Exe is a wide estuary at high water, giving a main race course area of a rough rectangle measuring two miles by one mile, with an extra mile of navigable channel towards the sea.

History

The report of the 'Fête Marine' of the 'Starcross Club' on 14th August 1775 is in Appendix I. It describes several yachts sailing from Starcross down to Teignmouth and back, as a squadron, as was then the custom. Though this is the first report, the club was actually formed on the 8th July 1772 by Lord Courtenay and Sir Lawrence Palk, 'both yachtsmen', with other members of the nobility, gentry and clergy.

It is not clear if a regatta took place each year, but certainly there were regular dinners. There were probably interruptions during the Napoleonic Wars, but there are very regular reports from about 1834 onwards in the *Flying Post*, which stopped publication in 1913. 1914 to 1922 were low years for the club and from 1922 until 1933, it amalgamated with the Checkstone Sailing Club nearby. Then it reappeared as the Starcross Yacht Club, using a small building on the shore in the village of Starcross to aid the sailing and racing, though the main gathering place was the Courtenay Arms Hotel, a short distance away. These places were evacuated in 1957, as mentioned above, with the establishment in the Earl's estate of the new building.

One reason that arrangements had to be changed in 1957, was the gradual decline of the old heavy wooden boats. A local class, the Starcross Viking was one of these; another was the National (West of England) Redwing, a clinker built 14 footer. These racers had lain on moorings off the shore, but they were being replaced by modern racing dinghies, which were stored ashore and launched for each race. Further progress with the even newer clubhouse is described above.

Classes
Lark, Laser, Mirror, Seafly, Solo, Portsmouth Yardstick, small cruisers.

Events and regattas
Racing never stops all year round, with weekend and mid-week racing from April to October and Sundays only in the remaining months. There are open meetings for the specific classes and handicap racing every week. There are trophies for all seasons and courses and even a Boxing Day trophy. The annual dinner-dance is in November. Also in November is an annual service at Powderham Church for all local sailing clubs. A junior section makes journeys to race at other clubs and in early November has a bonfire and fireworks. The cruiser section has several coastal races.

Members
360 : Patron: The Rt Hon The Earl of Devon

Address
Clubhouse, Powderham Point.
✆ 0626 890470
Postal address: General Secretary, Mrs Legood, Quarrylands, Little John's Cross Hill, Exeter, Devon, England.
✆ 0392 74387

England's oldest yacht club? Buildings of the Starcross YC today.

Royal Windermere Yacht Club

England's largest fresh water lake is of modest size by European standards. Measuring about ten miles long and less than one mile wide, Windermere is in the north-west of the country in the 'Lake District', an area of steep hills, lakes, streams and superb countryside, as well as considerable annual rainfall. There are islands on the lake and in the summer a steamer runs a service. Inevitably there are demands on it by all kinds of water user. The club has been 'royal' since 1887, an unusual honour in England for one situated away from salt water. The club possesses one of the last thriving formula classes in the world.

Clubhouse

The present clubhouse was built in 1965 on the site of previous ones, by the shore of the lake in the town of Bowness-on-Windermere; that is the only town of any size and is half way along the length of the lake. In the mid-1980s, the club was extensively refurbished. Adjoining is purpose laid out dinghy parking and there are rebuilt jetties into the lake.

Waterside

Six piers or jetties give temporary alongside berthing. The keeled classes lie on swinging moorings off the club and there are launching ramps for the racing dinghies. Bowness Bay Marina is adjoining.

History

The Windermere Sailing Club was formed in 1860 to give racing for sailing yachts not exceeding 25ft (7.6m) which were given club handicaps. A few years later the club introduced its own restricted class of 20ft (6.1m), but in 1871 a rule cheater design effectively killed off the class. After several attempts at other classes, a 22ft (6.7m) with low freeboard, bowsprit and lots of sail (gaffs and topsails) proved successful with the members. It usually carried two paid hands. There was betting on the races and crowds gathered to watch major regattas at the Ferry Hotel and on steam launches. An additional dinghy class with one sail was started in 1887, one of the boats, still surviving after a hundred years is still winning, sometimes on handicap.

In 1904, though the 22ft class was active, a new 17ft (5.2m) class (the length was on the waterline), again with restricted rules, so that designs were all slightly different, was created by the club. By 1914, for one reason and another, the 22s had died out and the 17s, with amateur crew only, remained. In 1920 a new 19ft (5.8m) design came in, with the proviso that no more of the 17 footers should be built, but it ended in 1934; the members preferred the 17s. From 1934 there was a boom in building 17s which were developing to look like 6-metres of the time with Bermudan rig, long main boom and double spreaders. Lady members had been admitted since 1906 and there were several keen women helmsmen. Numbers of starters were probably up to twenty-five.

During the 1930s, a motor boat club started on the lake; racing marks were laid jointly by the two clubs. When Sir Henry Seagrave, attempting to break the world water speed record in 1930, was killed at 100 mph with his mechanic on the lake in *Miss England II*, the club cancelled its races the next day. In 1932, electricity was installed in the clubhouse.

After 1945, sailing was slow to revive, but the club adopted one-design racing dinghies which were modern for the time, the National Firefly in 1948 and the National GP Fourteen in 1951. As the 17s could be built to the restricted class rule, they gradually re-emerged using modern design and building techniques; in the 50s, designs by David Boyd were favoured.

In 1963, the International Flying Fifteen class was adopted by the club. In 1970, the International Soling was adopted, but discontinued in 1982. The Firefly disappeared in 1979, in favour of the International Laser. The Mirror arrived in 1975 and was adopted in 1980. In 1983, a new design for the 17 by Geoffrey Howlett made an appearance and 10 of these were in the class by 1992.

The monopoly position of the club in yachting on Windermere means that its history has been interestingly bound up with the progress of its racing classes. Its success is having a tight class structure, unlike many clubs which have been forced into nothing but handicap racing.

There have been royal visits; not always memorable! In 1927, the then Prince of Wales came ashore for tea at the club, on a tour of the district. *'Ordinary members were confined behind a rope. HRH drank his tea hastily and restlessly, signed a photograph and left'*. In 1957 the Queen and Prince Philip, were to review the club fleet from a steamer: dark cloud shrouded the fine hills, rain poured down and squalls scattered the boats. In 1992, the Princess Royal, President of the RYA and a yachtswoman, visited the club in the more relaxed modern manner.

Events and regattas
A main social event each month from April to November, racing every weekend for all classes and mid-week during holiday periods, with Thursday evening racing throughout the summer. Open meetings (entries by class owners from elsewhere) occur at least once each season for each class. There are more than fifty trophies for the various classes awarded for all kinds of successes.

Classes
Royal Windermere 17 footer (about 26ft (7.9m) LOA), unique class of 35 boats; International Flying Fifteen, 40 boats; GP14, 30; Laser, 40; Mirror, juniors only, 20. (Class activity rises and falls: for instance in 1992, the Flying Fifteens (designed 1946) increased by 6.

Members
500 : Hon Life Commodore from 1981, C.P.Crossley, born 1902.

Address
Fallbarrow Road, Bowness-on-Windermere, Cumbria, LA23 3DJ, England.
℡ 09662 3106

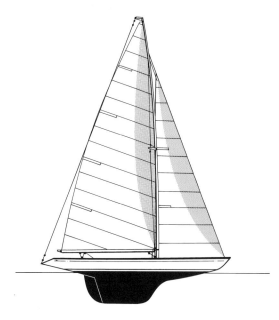

The Royal Windermere 17, current of the individual classes, chosen over the years by the club. The boats vary, being designed to a formula rule.

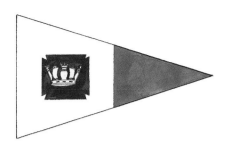

Royal Cruising Club

This is a club with no clubhouse, but many members who own boats and sail them considerable distances. There are relatively few members and the organization shuns publicity; seldom is there any mention of the RCC in the yachting press. On the other hand, the club publishes an annual hardback book, often over 300 pages, on sale to the public, under the title *Roving Commissions*. It is full of the accounts of cruises by members. They will be seen to be in a great many parts of the world. There is a strong social element, in Britain second possibly only to the Royal Yacht Squadron, proposers of candidates being asked if they would be prepared to spend long hours at sea with them. One is expected to feel at ease with any other member on shore at a club dinner. Most, though not all, of the members are British; there are continuing links with the Cruising Club of America, the Clyde Cruising Club and the Irish Cruising Club.

Clubhouse

As already mentioned, there has never been a clubhouse, but the members have the exclusive use of two rooms in a separate part of the Royal Thames Yacht Club in London. These rooms were until 1992 occupied by the International Yacht Racing Union. There have previously been similar rooms in London clubs or hotels.

History

The Cruising Club (it became Royal in 1902) was founded by nine men in December 1880. The leading spirit was Arthur Underhill, a lawyer, who went on to be commodore from 1888 to 1937. He felt in 1880 that *'upwards of twenty royal clubs should exist for the encouragement of racing, while the increasing class which was far more interested in cruising and navigation, was left entirely unrepresented'*. (It should be remembered that the racing in those days was round buoys and usually close inshore).

Among the rules were *'Any amateur is eligible for membership...the candidate for membership is a fit and proper person...refusal of the rules..or conduct unworthy of a gentleman ..shall render the member liable to expulsion by the vote of a majority...'* The rules have seldom been changed: in 1893, the concept of prizes for fine cruises was added and in modern times a more general clause states *'the prime object of the club has now (undated) become the furtherance of the best aspects of cruising under sail throughout the world in accordance with the highest traditions of the sea'*.

By 1901, the club had a membership of 173 with 113 yachts and 63 *'boats and canoes'*. It seems the yachts were small in the early days, an award being given, for instance for a circumnavigation of Ireland in thirty-three days (1896) by a 23ft (7.0m) waterline cutter owned by Dr Howard Sinclair. Other cruises went down the English Channel or across to the Baltic. Membership grew rapidly so that in 1904, a rule was passed to limit the membership to 250 (for modern limit see below). In 1906 a member whose small half decked yawl had been sailed across the North Sea and then dragged anchor off the German naval base of Jade was arrested and questioned for two hours. The RCC commodore protested to the foreign office and a diplomatic flurry ensued. It ended with the German authorities declaring the matter closed, expressing admiration for the adventurous sailor, but refusing to apologize as he had shown poor seamanship, spoke no German and had no papers of any sort.

One famous member (nothing to do with the above incident) was Erskine Childers (born 1870), whose classic of fictional cruising, *The Riddle of the Sands*, has remained in print since publication in 1903. Among his numerous cruises, it was his voyage to the Baltic in the 30ft (9.1m) cutter *Vixen* in 1897, which was the basis for the book. In 1910 he left the British civil service to devote himself to (Irish) politics and in 1914 was involved in a gun running incident in his 43ft (13.1m) ketch, *Asgard*. After serving in the British navy in the war, Childers became involved in the Irish negotiations and then joined in the civil war in Ireland against the new Free State government. At this stage he was asked to resign from the RCC. He was executed by an Irish Free State firing squad (not by the British as is sometimes thought) having been found carrying arms, in November 1922.

In about 1924, the club had to decide whether to lend its support to running an ocean race. The Cruising Club of America which had recently been formed on the lines of the RCC, decided to run the New London to Bermuda race (and has done so ever since). When in imitation of this a race around the Fastnet Rock was proposed in the press, the club was not sure. Claud Worth, a senior member and famous cruising man and author, suggested a race to Vigo instead; there is considerable correspondence from him on record setting out the objections to a Fastnet course. A member of the club, George Martin, had resigned from the club in 1921, having failed to be elected rear commodore. He took part with his Le Havre pilot cutter in the first Fastnet Race in 1925 and at its end formed a small group of the competitors to create the Ocean Racing Club (later the RORC, page 71). He was the first commodore of the latter.

Long distance cruising for small yachts began in the 1920s and early pioneers were club members George Mulhauser sailing around the world in *Amaryllis* and Ralph Stock in *Ogre* (he later wrote *Cruise of a Dream Ship*). Conor O'Brien in the 42ft (12.8m) *Saoirse* sailed round the world eastward and was one of the first yachtsmen to pass Cape Horn.

In later years the famous names that carried the club burgee were too numerous to enumerate here. There was Roger Pinckney (*Dyarchy*), Eric and Susan Hiscock (*Wanderers I* to *V*), Henry Denham (pilotage books and a vital role in the 1941 sinking of *Bismark*), Arthur Ransome, Bill Tilman, Peter Pye, Miles Smeeton. But there are so many names, so many yachts, so many outstanding voyages.

Classes
There are no classes, as there is no racing. The vast majority of members' vessels are between 32 and 50 ft LOA (9.7 and 15.2m).

Events and regattas
There is an annual dinner in March and monthly dinners in London in the winter months. There are three summer meets in England, where yachts can rally: May on the east coast, June in the south-west, September in Beaulieu River on the south coast. There are occasional foreign meets such as Hankö, Norway in 1987, Horta, Azores in 1989 and Douarnenez, France in 1992.

The annual awards by the RCC carry considerable prestige. The principal ones are the Royal Cruising Club Challenge Cup (1896) and the Romola Cup (1909). For cruises under one month there are the Founders' Cup and Claymore Cup. Other awards include the Seamanship Medal, Ladies' Cup, the Goldsmith Exploration Award, the Tilman Medal (for polar region cruises) and there are awards for young people.

Members
There is a limit of 400, which is fully subscribed. Minimum age for election is twenty-five. There are 250 extra members in categories such as Honorary, Senior, Naval and Associate. As there are about 400 yachts owned, it appears that most members are also owners.

Address
60 Knightsbridge, London, SW1X 7LF, England.

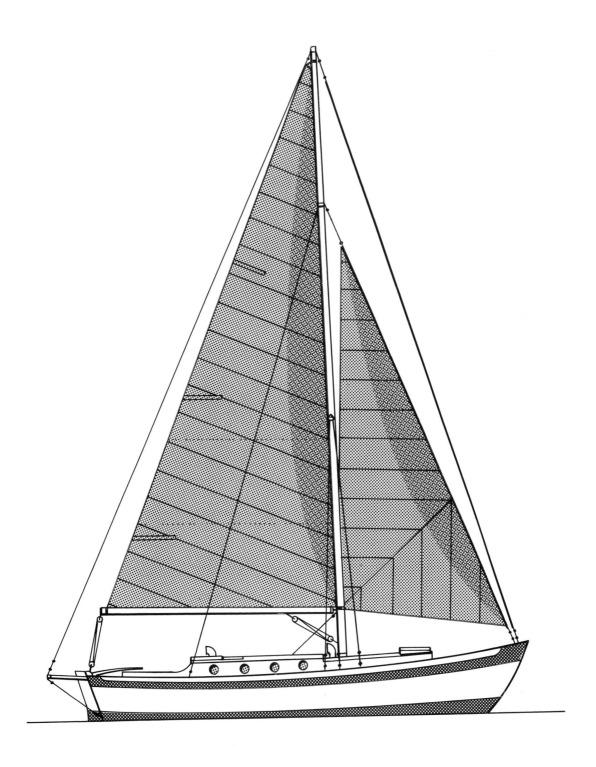

A boat which for many years was the essence of the Royal Cruising Club: *Wanderer III* owned by members Eric and Susan Hiscock from 1952 to 1968. They voyaged extensively, including twice round the world.

Cruising Yacht Club of Australia

Despite its name, the Cruising Yacht Club of Australia is famous for organizing races and its members' success in several of the great ocean racing classic of the world. It is certainly not one of the oldest yacht clubs in Australia, where the Royal Hobart Regatta was held in 1827 and yacht clubs formed in the 1830s. Of existing clubs, the Royal Yacht Club of Victoria was founded in 1853 and the Royal Sydney Yacht Squadron in 1862. Today the Cruising Yacht Club of Australia is among the leading ones. It declares that it is *'influential in the world'* and this claim is very true.

Clubhouse

The large clubhouse has been continuously improved and expanded since starting on the site of a boatshed in Rushcutters Bay within the world's largest natural harbour, Sydney, New South Wales. There are large verandahs and the dining room has a view over the harbour. The use to which these are put can be imagined from the function of 'Sunday morning breakfast on winter Sundays', where crews and families join and those not sailing have 'brunch' with 'a bottle of bubbly' on the sun deck. In 1991 there was not one wet morning in sixteen Sundays. Phew! Bar trading in a recent year was reported to have a profit of $A 85,000 (about £42,000 or $60,000). The club was rebuilt and extended most recently in 1985. A sailing school adjoins the club.

Waterside

A massive complex adjoins the club. There is a marina with 180 berths, ten visitor berths and thirty moorings. Another seventy-five berths are in an adjoining commercial marina. There are also small keel-boat moorings. A dinghy pontoon and boat racks are available for members and cradle slipway, mast crane, shipwright, chandlery, yacht broker, hardstanding for keel-boats.

History

The club was formed in 1944 for cruising yachts and in 1945 a cruise in company was planned from Sydney to Hobart, Tasmania, over the mid-summer Christmas holiday. However Captain J.H.Illingworth RN, finding himself stationed in Sydney at the end of World War II bought a 35ft (10.7m) yacht, *Rani*, joined the club and said that he was coming along, but could it be made a race?

Rani won this first race and as the distance was almost the same as the two international races of that time, the Bermuda and the Fastnet, the Sydney to Hobart became established as the third equal of these classics.

In 1965 the club sent a three boat team to England to compete for the first time as Australia in the Admiral's Cup (see page 71). The team did well; in 1967, a team was again sent and won the series, beating Great Britain and the United States (and six other countries), which up to then had a duopoly on the Cup. The Australian team was again the winner in the infamous Fastnet storm of 1979. In 1967, the club instituted an Australian version of the Admiral's Cup, known as the Southern Cross, for three boat international and Australian state teams. This has run biennially since.

Back in Sydney, the number and variety of offshore and shorter races, increased year by year into today's intensive programme (see below). The club has not been backward in enlisting commercial sponsors for events and even for individual boats, especially when these have to be sent to Europe or America. Yacht clubs usually ban the use of premises for business, but unusually the CYCA actually encourages members to use it for business lunches.

Classes
Ocean racer, cruiser-racer (rated on IMS, IOR, Performance Handicap System, JOG TCF)

Events and regattas
Most social occasions are held in conjunction with major or series events, of which the most important are the 603-mile Sydney-Hobart, starting on every Boxing Day (26 December); Sydney-Southport; Asia/Pacific ocean racing championships; summer twilight racing series; Sunday winter series in Sydney Harbour. A biennial event is Sydney to Noumea. There are numerous courses within the Harbour starting and finishing in Rushcutter's Bay and some immediately outside. Many races are in conjunction with the Middle Harbour YC, the Royal Prince Alfred YC, the Royal Prince Edward YC and the Royal Sydney Yacht Squadron. The summer season opens with a race on 1st September and concludes with the Easter regatta in April. Winter season racing runs from late April to the beginning of August.

Members
1,500 : Including a number of leading offshore sailors from overseas. Australian sailing remains male dominated and there are no ladies on the main committee, nor as sub-committee chairman. The exception is a special women's committee (at one time headed by the commodore's wife!) which appears to busy itself with things like a fashion parade, Christmas decorations, cleaning the cups and manning the telephones and reception desks for the big races.

Address
New Beach Road, Darling Point, New South Wales, 2027, Australia.
✆ 02 363 9731

The dock of the CYCA.

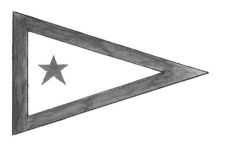

San Diego Yacht Club

Situated in one of the three major cities of the west coast of the United States of America, the club's greatest moment in history was when its yacht, skippered by its own commodore, Dennis Conner, in 1987 won the *America*'s Cup off Fremantle, Australia. As a result, the next defence (in fact, the next three, at this writing) was by the San Diego Yacht Club. In a way, it was not so much taking it from Australia, as the transferring of the defence to the Pacific rim, that is significant. In this work on yacht clubs, it must be reflected how the 'holy grail' of yacht racing originated in England, spent most of its life being raced in New York and Newport, RI, and then came to the Pacific.

Clubhouse
Successive clubhouses (see below) have been afloat or built out over the water and the present one dates from 1961, when the club was stretched financially to construct it. It was an excellent investment and within a few years further improvements were in hand to slipways and adjoining land.

The club, at Point Loma by the attractive suburb of Shelter Island, has driveways and gardens, but also has balconies and sundecks over the water, then docking and marina berths. There are tennis courts, swimming pool, picnic area, sail drying area. Public rooms are plentiful, including restaurant, bar, coffee shop, snack bar and open and spacious in this all the year round sailing port, close to the border of Mexico at only 32 degrees 40 minutes north. One hundred employees maintain the club and serve members and guests.

Waterside
500 marina berths and visitor berths for short stay adjoin club, hard standing for keel-boats, launching slips and alongside docking for launching keel-boats and dinghies. Four hoists to 8,000 lb (3,628 kg).

History
In 1885 in San Diego, the whaling station was removed from Ballast Point and the Santa Fé railroad reached the port. The result was increased prosperity and water space for leisure and the San Diego Rowing Club was formed in 1886, swiftly followed by the yacht club in the same year. The club moved into a lighthouse keeper's house at Ballast Point until it was taken over by the military with the Spanish-American War of 1898. In 1903 another clubhouse was occupied, but only for two years.

Sir Thomas Lipton was in the habit of presenting magnificent cups to clubs all over the USA (which perhaps helped the sales of tea) and the furthest of all from New York was the San Diego Lipton Cup of 1903. It seems to have been used for the defence of a match race challenge won by a Herreshoff 47ft (14.3m) sloop, *Detroit*, from the Great Lakes. In 1905 the San Diego YC and the (local) Corinthian Yacht Club merged and the dues were raised from 50 cents to one dollar per month, with dire warnings that this would mean the demise of the club. The burgee adopted for the combined clubs was that of the latter and this is the one in use today.

In the same way that a crown is a common symbol in a number of European and other countries that are monarchies, so the five-

The clubhouse and just a few
of its members' yachts.

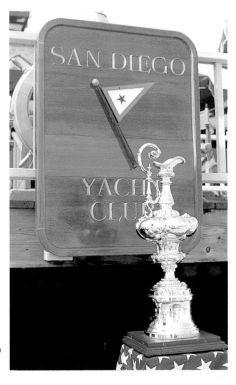

The club holds the *America's* Cup
against all others.

pointed star is one of the frequently seen symbols in yacht club heraldry in the USA.

Before 1914 membership was about 120; a 100 ft (30.5m) ex-ferry, ex-dance hall became the clubhouse and was afloat at the bottom of Hawthorne Street. From this club was run the annual schedule of twenty-three races between May and September, a lot for those days, when the idea of year round sailing did not exist in any country and those taking part

still worked long hours at office or factory. From 1918 onwards, the Navy and Army became conspicuous in San Diego. In the 1920s boom, yachting expanded and a record 112 boats were entered in a major regatta hosted by the club: that of the Southern California Yachting Association and the Pacific Coast Yachting Association.

Meanwhile the club had moved into yet another new clubhouse at Coronado. This was moved in one piece by barge in 1934 to an infilled site at Roseville Pier.

A thriving class was the R-class racing keel-boat of about 38ft (11.6m), which cost about $8,000 (rated to the Universal Rule). It closely resembled the European 6-metre (of the International Rule). The Stock Market crash of 1930 saw the end of the class with boats then changing hands for $500. When the economy revived, the east coast sailors had agreed with the Europeans to change over to 6-metres and the International Rule, leaving the Universal Rule for the J-class (*America*'s Cup) only. The R and similar P and Q classes in the USA died out. One-designs took over and the club was conspicuous in its members winning Star Class national championships. The Junior section, created in 1929, raced Penguins.

After 1945, the Lipton Cup was allocated to the Star class and in 1947, the San Diego to Ensenada Race began, attracting the biggest entry of cruiser-racers, year after year, in America. Other offshore racing included courses from the San Diego to Honolulu and Acapulco. By 1957 offshore racing was in the ascendancy and the boats were organized under the old CCA (Cruising Club of America) rating rule as the San Diego YC Racing Fleet. As in so much of America and elsewhere, the boats became bigger and the courses and their destinations more exotic. In 1962, with a membership of 975, the old clubhouse was cut in half and moved inshore on club ground and reassembled and today's clubhouse was constructed.

In the 70s the world grew ever closer and the 'distant' club, was sailing the same IOR boats as the rest of the world with a local designer, Doug Peterson, making an international name for himself in Ton Cup and Admiral's Cup designs in Europe, the Mediterranean and the SORC of Florida. Offshore races from San Diego were reprogrammed with the Manzanillo instead of Acapulco. Heavy involvement with the *America*'s Cup began in 1974 with Gerry Driscoll skippering *Intrepid* and Dennis Conner navigating *Courageous*. The latter became commodore of the club in 1984 and that very year won the club's Lipton Cup.

Classes
International Etchells 22 (approx 30), PC (32ft (9.75m) wood sloop, International Star (more class champions claimed than any other club), Lehman 12, 8ft Sabot. For Junior training Laser, Laser 2 and Flying Junior.

Events and regattas
For reasons well known, this club has become the defender of the *America*'s Cup, still yachting's greatest and with an historic place in international sport. The cup was successfully defended in 1988 and 1992; it was due to be sailed there again in 1995; it has be held in San Diego waters and it is a club which is always the defender. If the New York Yacht Club, or any other United States club is ever again to be the defending club, the series will first have to be won by a foreign club and then the NYYC win it back from there. For that reason, there is negligible support in the defence from other American clubs.

Among regular events are the Lipton Cup (late spring), *Yachting* (magazine) cup for the large fleet which returns from Mexico after the Newport Beach (Ca) to Ensenada Race, the Hot Rum series (three Sundays in November). There is a biennial race of 1,100 miles to Manzanillo, Mexico.

There is an all year round social programme and sailing for ocean racing classes (PHRF), Stars and Junior classes. In 1992 the Formula One commercial ODs held a regatta.

A strong junior programme, with about 200 between ages of 7 to 18 race each weekend, fifty participating parents, ten instructors: ten week summer season plus winter weekends. The result has been many successes in junior national and international racing.

Members
1,800 : A number of top international professionals have originated in the membership including Dennis Conner, Lowell North, John Driscoll and Gary Weisman. Joe Jessop who was commodore in 1929 was still sailing in Wednesday afternoon races in 1993. Two-thirds of the membership own boats.

Address
1103 Anchorage Lane, San Diego, California, 92106, USA.
℡ 0101 619 222 1103

Seawanhaka Corinthian Yacht Club

This club stated to the author *'We were the first Corinthian yacht club in the world'*. Also a recent commodore said *'Seawanhaka's tradition is second to none. When I joined, to be active in yachting, one had to be a member of Seawanhaka. Today it is not the case because of broadened participation in international yachting by many clubs.'* So here we have one of those select clubs that led yacht racing for decades before the proliferation of international classes, rules and fixtures.

The club has always been in Oyster Bay on Long Island, with its own protected anchorage and all the waters of Long Island Sound on which to race, not to mention close by the shore in even more protected waters. It is one of the those 140 clubs on the Sound (see Larchmont YC, page 67), but surely everyone would admit that the Seawanhaka was unusually senior and distinguished. The number of members is limited.

Clubhouse

The clubhouse with its imposing colonial style frontage in its own leafy grounds is the original building of 1892 and has apparently changed little on the outside. It has every facility one would expect for a select membership in the New York area. By road one drives out into Long Island and makes for the village of Oyster Bay. The immediate surroundings are mainly the private estates of affluent dwellings; this is within commuting range of Manhattan.

Waterside

There is no marina, which would spoil the lush surroundings, but there are short stay berths alongside at floats (pontoons). Yachts lie at swinging moorings in Oyster Bay Harbor. There is extensive hard standing for the big fleet of keel-boats; they are both dry sailed and laid up here in the winter. Though the inlet which is 'the Bay' curls around, the total distance from its mouth to the end is about three miles. Cold Spring Harbor, an adjoining inlet running south east from the open Sound is about four miles long and one mile wide.

History

Any club which publishes two fat volumes of its history and has the first actually finishing in 1897, must have a bit of a story to tell. Even the RYS (page 63) has its first volume going to 1900.

Despite the comment above, the term 'Corinthian' was being bandied about in England, though it does seem that no British club inserted the word into its name before 1871. That was the year when half a dozen yacht owners met on board a schooner in Oyster Bay and formed 'The Seawanhaka Yacht Club of Oyster Bay'. The objects were to regularize racing which was already happening in the area and make it all-amateur, without paid crew. The early meetings of the club were held on a schooner in summer and a member's house or at an hotel in New York city in the winter.

Essentially the racing was for small yachts, in contrast to the New York Yacht Club, most boats in the races being between about 20 and 35 feet (6.0 and 10.7m). For a decade the club expanded in membership and yachts. The races had been given the titles of 'Corinthian' courses, but the club did not

The fine clubhouse and surroundings of the Seawanhaka Corinthian YC.

insert the word into its title until the general meeting in New York of 10th January 1882; the present name was there adopted. Apparently the proposal had been rejected by the club members in 1874. (It has to be said that the Royal Corinthian Yacht Club, now of Burnham-on-Crouch and Cowes, England, claims to have been formed at Erith near London in 1872, as the Corinthian Yacht Club. There is still a road at the site called Corinthian Manor Way.)

In 1891 the club made a full investigation of the immediate coastline with a view to fixing a permanent clubhouse. As with so many of these early clubs in America and Europe, the arrival of an efficient railroad was a major factor. When the Long Island Railroad was connected with Oyster Bay, combined with unsuitability of other stations and an amalgamation with the existing Oyster Bay YC, the present site was bought and the clubhouse, which exists today was opened at a big ceremony ashore and afloat on 27th May 1892. Thereafter Oyster Bay, Centre Island and this part of Long Island Sound became, without ceasing, one of the world's major yacht racing stations.

The Seawanhaka Cup. The SCYC played a major part in the development of yacht racing and rating rules for many years. There is no space to detail this role here, but starting in 1895, there began an international match race for the famous Seawanhaka Cup. Very small keel-boats (less than 25ft, 7.6m) came from England to compete, a very unusual occasion at that time. It was necessary to create a rule of rating for the matches and this became the Seawanhaka rule. The influence of this rule was profound on all yacht racing, partly because the rule became combined with others on both sides of the Atlantic, being a component of the RORC (page 71) rule in 1931 and subsequently the IOR (International Offshore Rule) in 1968. In later years the Seawanhaka Cup was given for International 6-metres in competition between different countries. This was very significant because the 6-metre was a European creation and the Seawanhaka was influential in establishing it in America.

By 1971 it was switched to Soling class keel-boats; this use of one designs gave fine regattas at Oyster Bay and brought sailors of a number of countries together, but it was no different to many other international races except by being for a cup with a distinguished history. This is confirmed by the remarks of a commodore mentioned above. When a British challenger won the cup from time to time (unlike the *America*'s Cup, there was no winning streak), the races were held in Scotland or the Solent.

Over the years a host of regional, North American and international class championships have been hosted by the SCYC: International 12, 8 and 6-metres, Dragons, Stars and many one-design classes. The club locally raced many classes from year to year which have come and gone; for instance in the 1920s there were the R and S classes to the Universal Rule which subsequently disappeared.

Classes
Main classes are the Shield and Sonar keel-boat one-designs. Others very active are International J24, Seabird, International Soling.

Events and regattas
In the fine surroundings, social events include the season opening day, Lobster cookouts, Wednesday night speakers and occasional dances. Among events for cruisers are the 50-mile overnight Stratford Shoal Race and the July two-day club rendezvous. Racing includes Fall regatta, district and North American championships for several classes, traditional team races against British clubs (Seawanhaka Cup, British-American Cup). Junior programme has produced American and Olympic champions. In the world of more professional yachting, club policy remains essentially Corinthian.

Members
Limited to 450. Honorary member: HM King Harald of Norway.

Address
Centre Island, Oyster Bay, NY11771, USA.
✆ 0101 516 922 6200

Royal Perth Yacht Club

In the burgee of the Royal Perth Yacht Club at Fremantle, Western Australia, it is only necessary to move the crown from the upper quarter to the centre of the red cross on white to be the same as the Royal Yacht Squadron. This is one of the three clubs in the world (the others are the New York YC and the San Diego YC, pages 55 and 88), to have held the *America*'s Cup, supreme trophy of the sport for over 140 years. In 1990 and 1994, it was the host to a stopover of the Whitbread Round The World Race.

In the RPYC sailing instructions for all races is the rule '*All white sailing dress with minimum of white shirt and shorts shall be worn by all competing crews. Yachts whose crews fail to comply may be scored "did not start"* '. Flag officers have uniforms displaying ranks.

Clubhouse
The main clubhouse is at Crawley in the Swan River suburb of Nedlands and within sight of the centre of the city of Perth. It adjoins the University of Western Australia and student's cars are to be found parked outside the club. The clubhouse was built in 1953 with major renovations in 1972 and 1981. There is a second clubhouse, 'an ocean annexe', built at Challenger Harbour, Fremantle, by the open sea in 1986, to cope with the season of the *America*'s Cup. Near here many of the *America*'s cup 12-metres were berthed. Both clubhouses have all the facilities expected of a leading Australian club with its virtual all the year round sailing. In a recent year the net profit of the bars was $A 80,000.

Waterside
At the main clubhouse there are marina berths for 320 and six short stay places for visitors, also dinghy launching slip, launching ramp and crane. At Fremantle there are thirty-five berths, ten for visitors and two cranes. At both club sites there is hard standing for members' yachts.

History
The Perth Yachting and Boating Club was formed in 1865, the oldest such organization in Western Australia. In 1880, the club's first jetty and boat shed were built at the bottom of William Street. There was no esplanade then and the tide surrounded the club at high water. In 1890 the royal warrant was granted, the word 'boating' dropped and the present title assumed. While the members hailed this, a local newspaper said (as happily quoted today by the club) '*Does the regal epithet apply to the city of Perth or to the yacht club? But really what nonsense it is , asking permission to dub a potty little yacht club in a fourth rate colonial city, that has not a ten tonner in its fleet, a royal club.*'

The *America*'s Cup is theoretically a contest between yacht clubs. Early Australian challenges came from Sydney, but in 1977 Alan Bond challenged from the Sun City YC. He first challenged through the Royal Perth in 1980, then again in 1983, when he won the cup 4 races to 3 in the best of 7. The club ran the 12-metre world championships in 1986. The club, represented by The Task Force 87 Syndicate (chairman Kevin Parry), defended the cup in 1987 off Fremantle and lost 0-4. Since 1982 the RPYC has run the Australia Cup, a nation-wide match racing contest. By

Royal Perth Yacht Club main building.

1993, the club had produced world champions in six classes and thirty-two national champions in various classes. In 1988 and 1993 the club ran a leg of the World Match Racing Championship that is heavily financed and sponsored and moves round major clubs of the world. In 1993 the club ran the final of this series in 36ft (11.0m) one-designs. Australian skippers are invariably well up each year in the resulting order.

Jon Sanders, who is a native of Perth, in 1986-88 sailed under the club burgee on his three times round the world voyage without stopping.

Classes
Cruiser-racer, offshore racer (IMS, IOR and YAH handicap), S80, S22, Endeavour 24, Etchells 22, Viking, M27 Thunderbird, Farr 9.2. Dinghy classes: Cherub, 420, Laser, Pelican, Junior Dinghy.

Events and regattas
Governor's cup, West Coast ocean racing series, Fremantle – Albany Race, ANZAC Day Digger's Cup, winter Olympic classes. Functions include Oktoberfest, Mothers' Day lunch, Melbourne Cup lunch, Mardi Gras ball.

Members
900 senior, 600 other categories; ladies are associate members. Patron: His Excellency the Governor of Western Australia (ever since foundation).

Address
P.O.Box 5, Nedlands, 6009 Western Australia.
✆ 619 389 1555

The RNSA, with major help from the Royal Navy, starts the Whitbread Round The World Race.

Royal Naval Sailing Association

This is one of the largest clubs in the world in terms of membership and claims to have more members than any other in the United Kingdom. The members are from all ranks of the Royal Navy, Royal Marines, retired Navy and Marines and some closely associated civilians. Here one must repeat that untrue saying that the most unhelpful items in a sailboat are 'a wheelbarrow, an umbrella and a naval officer'. The grain of truth in this was that army colonels or majors were often named as winning helmsmen in yachts, while the British Navy had abandoned sail training earlier than most of the world's navies long before World War I in its quest for modernization. Army clubs like the Royal Artillery Yacht Club and Royal Engineers Yacht Club, were earlier supporters of the first Fastnet Race. Some navy men on retirement follow the old formula and walk inland with an oar over their shoulder until someone asks what it is; others have been lifelong seaman who have cruised and raced thousands of miles in sailing yachts.

There is no clubhouse. The RNSA headquarters offices are in Portsmouth, Britain's principal naval port, where HMS *Victory* permanently lies with other historic ships. There are branches around the UK at Clyde, Forth, Medway, Plymouth, Portland, as well as Portsmouth. There is a branch at Gibraltar. Affiliated are a British Columbia Squadron, Sydney Squadron of the Royal Australian Navy and the Royal Marines Sailing Club. Throughout the world, there are appointed Honorary Local Officers of the association.

History

In August 1935 Vice Admiral Geoffrey Blake CB DSO presided over a meeting at which the Naval Sailing Association was formed. Six months later King George V (a noted yachtsman) approved the title 'royal'. By April 1936, there were 410 members and 93 privately owned yachts. The same year the association took part in the international naval races at Kiel and held a rally in the Solent. In 1937 the RNSA won the RORC interclub points shield for the season's ocean racing. The RNSA 14 ft dinghy was established; it was also 'the Island dinghy' (at Cowes), as a rugged clinker open sailing and racing boat and many of these were used in the British services for recreation and training up to the 1950s.

Post-war, Captain John Illingworth and others established an ocean racing one-design, the RNSA 24 (waterline, 7.3m), versions of which sailed all the major RORC and some overseas races, including the transatlantic race. Since 1965 the RNSA has sponsored the rugged, but modern, sailing dinghy, the Bosun, designed by Ian Proctor. It remains widely used by sailors, soldiers and airman: boats have been refurbished and replaced to last until the year 2000.

Classes

RNSA owned: 14 Lasers 1 and 2. Seamanship training (RN): 7 Contessa 38, 2 Sigma 38, 15 Victoria 34s (from 1990), 4 Nicholson 32s and some 30 others. Numerous other yachts including Nicholson 55s are part of joint service sailing. RN and RNSA have close arrangements on these. 18 sailing cruisers as 'recreational yachts'.

Events and regattas

From 1973 to 1994, the RNSA ran the Whitbread Round The World Race every fourth year. It usually starts in September in the Solent and was scheduled for 1993, 1997 etc. This race is increasingly professional, commercial and manned by sailing rock-stars, while the club is essentially an amateur one existing for the benefit of its members and service training. Soundings from time to time indicated continued support for the race from members. The RNSA supplied the chairman, medical advisers and the race director, now a permanent paid post. At the end of the 1994 race, the Association withdrew from the event.

The first race in 1973-1974 depended in a large measure for entries and for contacts in foreign ports on the British services; this changed as Whitbread took a bigger burden.

The Read Cup, named after a founder of the association, is sailed for whenever crews from the RN and USN ships meet and can set up a race: there is an accumulative points system. The Albion Trophy is a similar match with Canadian warships.

Dinghies and board sailing involve joint service championships and other matches. There is an annual services offshore regatta and Cowes Week rally and party. The training boats and the big joint service ones, such as the Nicholson 55, *Adventure*, which sailed in the early Whitbread races, cover thousands of miles every year, the latter having done many transatlantic and other passages in open water. Private cruising yachts manned by retired naval men, cover the world's oceans.

Members

7,300 : 4,025 privately owned vessels notified. The Admiral is HRH Prince Philip and the list of members distinguished in the world of yachting would be long.

Permanent honorary flag officers include Otto Steiner and Charles Williams (chairman of the Whitbread race for two and three times respectively), Erroll Bruce, pioneer ocean racer and Robin Knox-Johnston of numerous sailing feats including the first man ever to sail single-handed round the planet without stopping.

Address

Headquarters: 17 Pembroke Road, Portsmouth, Hampshire, PO1 2NT, England.
✆ 0705 822321

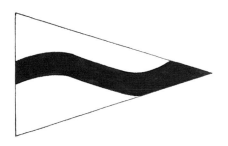

Cruising Club of America

The size of the USA means, that unlike Europe, there are very few clubs which expect to embrace the whole country. The CCA is however such a club and actually has 'stations' in various yachting ports. It was founded as a direct counterpart to the Royal Cruising Club (page 83), but has also had a kind of liaison with the RORC, described below.

Clubhouse and Waterside
There is no clubhouse or particular sailing waters. The oceans of the world are the cruising ground of members.

History
In the winter of 1921-22, a group of yachtsmen looking around the large yachting scene across the United States, saw that yacht clubs were invariably intended for the conduct of racing on closed courses and for social purposes. The previous season William Nutting, editor of *Motor Boat* magazine, had sailed to England in 1920 and then returned late in the year to the USA in a particularly stormy passage. One of the crew was Uffa Fox, who recounted the passage for posterity in his book *Sailing, Seamanship and Yacht Construction*. The 42ft (12.8m) ketch, *Typhoon,* was capsized but recovered.

Nutting had met senior members of the Royal Cruising Club (page 83), including Arthur Underhill and Claud Worth, in England. He decided to use the RCC as a model. The title Cruising Club of America was always intended to be wide ranging and not necessarily imply only the United States.

Almost immediately the CCA became involved in two major yachting projects, which remain important to this day. One was the Blue Water Medal and the other was the Bermuda Race.

A race from various east coast ports to Bermuda had been held six times between 1906 and 1923. After the 1923 race, those involved asked the newly formed CCA to take over the running, the finish being provided by the Royal Bermuda Yacht Club. This it has done ever since and the race is held in June on even numbered years; since 1936 the start has been at Newport, RI. For many years the race was considered the premier American ocean racing classic. Latterly, in common with many events, the vast number of races available makes it difficult to single out which are 'important'.

The club developed a rating rule in order to give time allowances in the race: the CCA rule. Although the CCA ran only this one race every two years (and ran two transatlantic races in the 1930s, but that is all), its rating rule became widely, though by no means universally used in both North and South America. In the 1960s the CCA worked with the British to combine its rule with that of the Royal Ocean Racing Club, used throughout Europe and the Far East. The result in 1970 was the IOR (International Offshore Rule).

From the CCA point of view this was never entirely satisfactory. The RORC was a quite different organization, wholly involved with racing and conducting many races every year. The CCA were essentially looking for fine (and rather bigger) cruising yachts. Many in Europe misunderstood this and believed it was an American equivalent of the RORC. In 1978 the fragile pact, which had lasted for just four races was broken and an extra rule called MHS was used as well as IOR. In 1980, after the Fastnet storm and fatalities, only the MHS was used. IOR was allowed back in later, but dropped after 1988. In England the RORC had used IOR only for the Fastnet until 1987. So from 1989/90 the clubs parted completely.

The Blue Water Medal has remained the world's foremost yacht cruising award. Unlike the RCC Challenge Cup, it is not confined to club members. The names of the winners and their boats since the first medal, which went to Alain Gerbault of France in *Firecrest* in 1923, reads like a roll of historic cruises. Though USA nationals have obviously won the medal most, there have also been thirteen from Britain, five from France and three from Sweden. In 1940 the Blue Water Medal was awarded to all British yachtsmen who aided the evacuation of the British Army and French soldiers from Dunkirk.

Events and regattas

Newport to Bermuda Race (615 miles) in June every even year. Various cruising awards in addition to Blue Water Medal, including Richard S. Nye Trophy, Circumnavigation Award, Vilas Literary Prize, Transoceanic Pennant. The CCA has established stations which organize their own meets, lectures and cruises. The stations are: Boston, Essex, New York, Chesapeake, Florida, Pacific North-West, San Francisco, Southern California, Great Lakes, Buzzards Bay, Gulf of Maine and outside USA, Bermuda and Nova Scotia.

Classes

Not applicable to huge range of members' cruising yachts. Bermuda Race by IMS racing, but classification traditionally is modified from race to race.

Members

1,100. Ladies cannot be members. This is more restrictive than the RCC 450, when compared by population. Commodore serves for two years in accordance with US short tenure custom. Eight rear commodores, one per important station. There is a fleet surgeon and fleet chaplain.

Address

Secretary, P.O.Box 4024, Boston, MA02101, USA
✆ 0101 617 951 7382

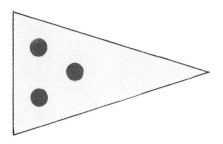

Imperial Poona Yacht Club

Yes, this club really exists. Its membership is as follows: United Kingdom 26, Bermuda 25, Hong Kong 25, USA 22. It has had one commodore since 1945 and he still (1993) holds the position. He is Sir Reginald Bennett VRD, a substantial character, who was for many years a member of Parliament; as such he is an accomplished and amusing speaker, a necessary asset in this particular club.

There is no clubhouse and no waterside.

History
The story of 'this great Imperial Foundation' is best told in the words of the official history. Some might judge it a send-up of all yacht clubs; others would say it distils the roots of all 'clubbiness'. So the history, as issued to members only, will be found at Appendix V, page 166.

The formation was on 22nd April 1934 and was (at that time) limited to fifteen members, male, who must be members of other yacht clubs and unmarried. The founders said that *'in the era of the Raj, many who served, whether in arms or as box-wallahs, have returned to these islands carrying with them the traditions, mores and speech of the great Sub-Continent'*. The rules led inevitably to a decline in membership: in 1938 with only three left, the club was dissolved. During these four years of existence, however, a series of matches and Tiffins took place *'and the club's colours were flown frequently in events in Imperial Waters on either side of the Atlantic'*.

In 1946, the club was reformed in England, abolishing the bar on matrimony and with twenty-five members. It also decided *'to recognize the national authority'* which policy remains today! Overseas branches followed.

In the USA in 1951 the Revolting Colonists Outpost was formed and in 1969 the Section Batards Normands was established in the Deauville Yacht Club, *'in memory of a local Duke who had cruised to Hastings in 1066'*.

Members are given names such as Oont Sahib and Imam of the Revolting Colonists, but the membership list remains confidential. 'The Maharaja Sahib' who attends some of the club's more exotic functions is said to be a senior member of the British Royal Family.

Events and regattas
The main fixture is for the Poona Pot, presented in 1956 by His Highness the Maharaja of Cooch Parwani. It was raced for many years at Cowes between the club and four other clubs at Cowes. There was one boat (a keel one-design) per club and in the first year, the skipper of the club entry was Uffa Fox. More recently keel-boats at other locations have been used. The event is not necessarily held every year and there can be five year intervals.

Members. 26 in the UK and 97 abroad (see above).
Past or present members: Charles E. Nicholson, Uffa Fox, Sir Alec Rose, Bus Mosbacher, Sherman Hoyt. Flag officers of the club besides the commodore are the Great White Vice, the Great Gorgeous Rear and the Colonel-in-Chief.

Address
of honorary secretary
Dr M. Green, 38 Lansdowne Gardens, London, SW8, England.
✆ 071 622 8286

Longest serving club commodore
(for 49 years) in the world?
Sir Reginald Bennett of the
Imperial Poona Yacht Club.

Naval 'cutters' at the
British Kiel Yacht Club.

British Kiel Yacht Club

Where the famous yachting waters of Kieler Forde narrow in the approach to the Nord-Ostsee Kanal and the city of Kiel itself, there are the narrows of Friedrichsort. Here a number of marinas and yacht harbours line both banks, including the massive concrete structures and attached marina built for the 1972 Olympic Games. To the west of this is the village of Stickenhorn. There are the club and yard building and marina berthing of a slight anachronism, the British Kiel Yacht Club.

It is a club for the recreational use of the British forces in Germany, but scores of boats from many nations call at the club every year. Usually they are on their way to or from the Nord-Ostsee Kanal (the Kiel Canal), which connects the North Sea and the Baltic (the 'East Sea').

Clubhouse
A complex of buildings immediately adjoins the marina at Stickenhorn. The club is concerned with the maintenance of the yachts and has accommodation for members of the forces who have come to sail. The original clubhouse, which was that of the Kiel Yacht Club was vacated and returned to its owners, as described below.

Waterside
Marina and bows-to berthing for all club yachts and for visitors; the latter are frequent because the club is on the route between the Baltic and England (and western European coast)

History
When Colonel W.G.Fryer, a senior officer of the Royal Engineers, arrived in at the old Olympia Haven, after the German surrender in 1945, he found it *full of yachts and the Kieler Yacht Club locked up and empty. So I told the Chief Engineer and the AQMG of 8 Corps that I was going to requisition some yachts from the harbour and form a yacht club. They both nodded, so I went ahead.*' So the club came into existence on 11th June 1945. When the British, by air and ground, scoured the surrounds of Kiel for yachts and found several laid up in creeks and backwaters, some thirty-four cruiser-racers were seized and based at the club. They ranged from three 300 square metres, including *Nordwind*, 100 squares, 80s, 60s, 50s and others. From other parts of Germany, the British forces sailed many German service yachts, particularly 100 square metres and 50 square metres, to England, where they were sailed for many years. Also in Kiel were Stars, Sharpies and small boats. A dozen 30 square metres were used elsewhere in the Baltic and came to Kiel in 1950.

The British officers remembered the long established Kieler Woche, Kiel Week (which the Kaiser had begun in 1882 in imitation of Cowes Week). So they organized the first post-war Kiel Week at the beginning of September 1945 and it even ended with a firework display. *'The performance was made doubly spectacular by the accidental ignition of the complete stock in one of the landing craft'*. In 1946, Kiel Week saw visiting teams from Denmark, Holland and Norway; Germans were not yet in evidence socially, but local staff maintained the yachts. Some of the bigger yachts actually had their old paid hands who stayed with the boats.

Six years after the end of the war, in late 1951, the British Kiel Yacht Club moved out of the old Kieler Yacht Club, which was returned to German yachtsmen, and into buildings along the shore at Stickenhorn. At the same time all the private yachts which had been requisitioned were given back to their owners in better condition than they could have managed in the circumstances of the time. A charter fee for the time the boats had been taken from them was paid for each. The yachts seized in 1945 from the German armed forces have been kept indefinitely: some still sail today.

In the years that followed, the club became a busy sailing training base for British forces in Germany. A number of the old German pre-war yachts (wooden of course) were no longer seaworthy, so new yachts (glass fibre) were bought in England. In the 60s the Cutlass class was purchased, in 1971; the then new Contessa 32; in 1978 a fleet of Contessa 28s arrived. In effect the users had all the advantages of cruiser-racer one-design fleets. In 1988 the time came again to re-equip and a number of boats around 29ft (8.84m) were tested over a period. The winner was the German Hallberg-Rassy 29 (over British and French yachts).

For many years two personalities devoted their lives to the club. One of these was Lt Col Stan Townsend MBE, who, in vital club roles, such as Captain of Boats, trained officers and soldiers. On retirement from the Army he bought the 54ft (16.46m) *Ragna R*, loaning it continuously for training cruises. The other was Herr Bruno Splieth MBE. He came to the club after discharge from the German navy in a prisoner-of-war camp in 1945 (after heroically ferrying refugees from the east in the closing weeks of the war and then turning himself in at Kiel). From then until 1982 he was essential as Sailing Master, Yacht Master, Harbour Master, while he represented Germany in several Olympic Games and was on the German Olympic committee: a number of awards were made to him by German sailing, while the British recommended the Queen to make him an MBE. He passed on his knowledge and standards to thousands of British serviceman, who sailed at Kiel.

Classes
12 Hallberg-Rassy 29s, 5 Sigma 33s, 6 family cruisers. Yachts from England and elsewhere belonging to the forces are based at Stickenhorn from time to time.

Events and regattas
The official purpose of the club today is to provide yachts, equipment and spares for the Kiel Training Centre, an Army unit. There is weekend racing, charter of cruisers to servicemen and families and service regattas. The club is self financing and not a charge on the tax-payer. The land on which it stands is now the property of the German Federal Navy. Visiting yachts of all nations are welcome to berth at the BKYC, but capacity is limited.

Members
Membership is for the British armed forces under their own arrangements. The permanent members are the flag officers and staff of the operation.

Address
General secretary, British Kiel Yacht Club, Military Secretary's Branch, British Army of the Rhine, BFPO 140, Germany.
✆ 02161 47 22024

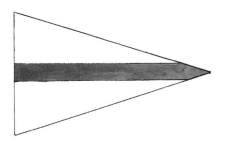

Nippon Ocean Racing Club

Because of geographical separation, yachting in Japan is not well reported in America and Europe. In fact from 1964, and earlier, when the yachting Olympics were staged at Enoshima, dinghy racing, class racing and ocean racing have expanded steadily. More recently wealthy corporations have been sponsors of boats in the Admiral's Cup, *America*'s Cup and Whitbread Round The World Race. The name is reminiscent of the Royal Ocean Racing Club in England; in Japan the Imperial family does not have a connection with any clubs, as do most European monarchies. A Japanese correspondent points out that yacht racing is an 'imported culture'.

Clubhouse
The office and club rooms are in Tokyo at the address below, but there are twelve branches at yachting stations throughout Japan.

History
In 1948 a number of foreigners in the occupying forces, or resident in Japan by nature of their current work, formed the Cruising Club of Japan, CCJ. The first offshore race was the Yokohama to Oshima in August 1950, the first ocean event since the war and this stimulated the Japanese membership of the club. The new members wanted to concentrate on racing and in January 1954, the CCJ was reorganized as the Nippon Ocean Racing Club.

The Ministry of Transport recognized the NORC as the national authority for offshore racing. Subsequently the club developed 'squadrons', eventually fourteen of them, from Hokkaido in the north to Okinawa in the south.

A major motive has been to compete with sailors from other countries and the club fielded teams in the RORC Admiral's cup in Britain in 1977, 1979 (the year of the Fastnet storm), 1983, 1989 and 1991 and 1993. The best result has been seventh, but the effort in getting three ocean racers and crews to the other side of the world has had to be considerable. From 1962 the club participated in the China Sea Race. Other strong competition has been offered by the club in the Southern Cross (Sydney) and the Kenwood Cup in Hawaii, since its inception in 1978. It ran the single-handed transpacific race in 1969, 1975 and 1981 and the double-handed race from Melbourne, Australia, to Osaka, which is unusual in being a south to north race sailing, not so much through time zones, as from autumn to summer (March, southern hemisphere to May, northern hemisphere); the course is 5,500 nautical miles. The club ran the 5,000-mile single-handed trans-Pacific race in 1969, 1975 and 1981. The Auckland to Fukuoka Race of 5,500 miles is a crewed event with stop-overs at Numea and Guam. The 1978, IOR Quarter Ton Cup (world championships) were run by the club in generally bad weather.

Classes
Japan is in an earlier cycle of ocean racing development than America and Europe, but equally technically advanced. In other words, there are classes that have been abandoned elsewhere, but also some that are bang up-to-date. Hence IOR classes, especially Two Tonners (45ft, 13.7m) and One Tonners (41ft,12.5m). IMS racers in 40 to 45ft range (12.2 to13.7 m) J-24s. 1,500 yachts of all kinds owned by members.

Events and regattas

Major and shorter ocean races including Okinawa Race and Toba Pearl Race; Japan Cup Race in even-numbered years. Regular trials and teams to Kenwood Cup (Hawaii) and Southern Cross trophy (within the Sydney to Hobart Race). Yamaha Osaka Cup in 1995.

Members

5,000

Address

2nd Sempakushinko Bldg, 1-11-2 Toranomon, Minato-ku, Tokyo 105, Japan.
℡ 03 3504 1991

Some boats of the substantial ocean racing fleet of the NORC, here competing for the 1992 Japan Cup, a regular event.

Ocean Cruising Club

Few clubs can be described as unique, but this may be one. As long distance ocean voyaging increased rapidly after 1945, it seemed to long distance sailor Humphrey Barton that none of the existing clubs met the needs of people like himself. An essential strand is drawn from the RORC (which needs a minimum offshore racing distance before joining), so that every member must have sailed at least 1,000 miles without stopping as skipper or crew in a vessel of under 70 ft (21.3m). Less than half the members are British (see below).

Clubhouse
There is no clubhouse, but there are some 90 'port officers' in the harbours of many countries, such as 14 in UK, 15 in USA, Australia (10), Caribbean (9), Canada (5), also Argentina, Brazil, Bermuda, Ireland, Israel, New Zealand, Portugal, Spain and Sri Lanka. The Royal Thames Yacht Club, London, 'extends a range of clubhouse facilities to OCC members'.

History
Humphrey Barton, a partner in the leading yacht design firm of Laurent Giles in England, was a leading sailor in the 1940s and 50s, writing books on ocean passages and voyaging and sailing long distances himself. When in 1954 he proposed a cruising equivalent of the RORC, the Ocean Cruising Club, essentially international and requiring a 1,000-mile passage qualification, it met a continuous response. The flying fish burgee and tie are among the best known of all yacht club symbols and, like the seahorse of the RORC, say something instantly about the person flying or wearing each.

It is simply impossible to recount the magnificent voyages of so many members. One can but resort to the cliché that this is a part of the yachting explosion of the second half of this century. Humphrey Barton was commodore from 1954 to 1960 and there have been five commodores since. From 1975 to 1982, it was Peter Carter-Ruck, the famous British libel lawyer and since 1989, it has been Mary Barton, widow of the founder, who continues to make long voyages. Over the years many of the members have also engaged in long-distance short-handed racing, generally considered to be closely related to ocean voyaging, rather than to 'racing round the buoys'. Like the Royal Cruising Club, a number of awards have gradually been introduced for different long distance cruising achievements.

Classes
There are no classes as there is no racing. Members appear to own 403 sailing yachts; 263 of these are between 27 and 42 ft (8.2 and 12.8m).

Events and regattas
Twice a year the OCC publishes for its members a compact journal of about 100 pages, under the title *Flying Fish*, with news of voyages, accounts of passages and letters from members. There are also such items as obituaries of famous members or ocean voyagers, remembering their activities of earlier years. This authoritative journal is important for the members who are by definition are scattered around the seven seas. There is also a quarterly newsletter and centralized cruising information service.

The chief annual award for members is the OCC Award. This is for the most outstanding contribution to the fostering and encouraging of ocean cruising in small craft and the practice of seamanship and navigation in all their branches. This seems quite a tall order. Other trophies are: the Barton Cup for the most meritorious voyage, the Rose medal for the most meritorious short-handed passage, the Rambler Medal for the best short voyage, the Water Music Trophy for the best cruising or pilotage information. For non-members, the Award of Merit is for person or persons who have recorded some outstanding achievement.

Every year there are a number of rallies and dinners. Typical events over an eighteen month period included yacht rallies in the Baltic at Helsinki; Smith's Cove, Penobscot Bay, Maine; Chesapeake Bay; Beaulieu River, England. In recent years a biennial pursuit race, with skippers endeavouring to predict exact required arrival time, such as midday Sunday 2nd August 1992 at Horta, Azores, has become instituted. For this a yacht can start from anywhere. There were annual dinners in London and Sydney, Australia.

Members
1,200 with a geographical spread: UK 520, USA (E) 319, USA (W) 56, Australia 97, Ireland 42, Canada 37, European continent 78, 48 in the rest of the world. As well as a commodore and vice commodore, there are rear commodores for Britain, USA(E), USA(W), Australia and three 'roving' ones, which sounds piratical.

Address
Secretary, P.O.Box 996, Tiptree, Colchester, Essex, CO5 9XZ, England.
℡ 0206 331108

Blackjack, a world cruiser of the 1990s which epitomizes the OCC; owned by Mike and Pat Pocock.

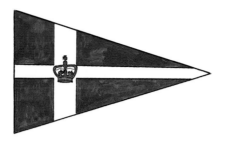

Royal Thames Yacht Club

The River Thames runs through London, but the members of this club never sail upon it. They did once. Among clubs, the Royal Thames has a strong claim to be one of the very oldest as discussed on page 15. Today it is essentially an excellent club with modern premises in the centre of London and an important annual sailing programme of races and regattas which take place in a number of venues around the coasts of Great Britain. In view of its location, the club is well known and used by many overseas visitors of the sailing world and for club, national and international conferences.

Clubhouse

This stands conspicuously in Knightsbridge, an exclusive area of London. The flag mast and yard arm give a breath of yachting as the heavy traffic snarls past day and night. There is a large dining room, bars on two floors, club rooms and meeting rooms. On the side away from the street, the greenery and gardens of Hyde Park are visible and the Household Cavalry with jingling harnesses ride past daily.

The building dates from 1963, following the demolition of the previous clubhouse on the site and the erection of a block, in which the third floor and upwards are commercial accommodation which have no connection with the club.

Until 1992, the International Yacht Racing Union had its offices in the Royal Thames on the ground floor; since then some of these rooms have been taken by the Royal Cruising Club (page 83). The clubhouse contains many fine cups and trophies dating from the 18th century onward and important paintings of sailing vessels and yachts. In the model room there is a remarkable collection of half models, which are a lesson in themselves on naval architecture.

Waterside

Since disposing of a substantial weekend house on the River Hamble on the south coast of England in 1980, the club now only has moorings at Hamble and Cowes. However there is a mobile race organization team with caravan and committee boats for regattas.

History

The story of this club is extensive because it has been a leading club of a leading yachting nation almost without interruption for 220 years – nearly a quarter of a millenium!

It is also well documented. The club has had twelve clubhouses or meeting places (full time houses were not the custom in the early days) since its foundation, all in central London. In 1775, the Duke of Cumberland, brother of King George III, gave a silver cup for a race on the River Thames for *pleasure sailing boats from 2 to 5 tons, lying above London Bridge*' and twenty boats entered. The winner was a yacht called *Aurora*, owned by Mr Parks, late of Ludgate Hill. Thus was begun the Cumberland Fleet or Sailing Society, as it was known until 1823, when it changed its name twice, the second time because a number of members broke away after a dispute about the finish of a race to form the Thames Yacht Club. The original club faded around 1827, while the break-away section became the Royal Thames in 1830, when its patron ascended the throne as King William IV.

By 1845, the club had 300 members including *'many noblemen and gentlemen of rank'* and *'nearly 150 yachts from 4 to 200 tons, some of them the fastest for their tonnage in the world, among others* Mystery, *winner of 14 cups in three years '* (which does not seem much today with our packed fixture lists). By this time the club had its own racing and right of way rules and its own tonnage rule for handicapping (Thames Measurement). Each important club had its own systems and national ones were unknown for another thirty-five years. Thames Measurement was used as a description of English sailing yachts quite widely until about 1960 and is even found occasionally today.

With the affluence that followed the Napoleonic Wars, the members' yachts became larger and the open seas became safe for sailing. For many years the club held races from committee boats in the Thames estuary, well below London and its docks, but by the late 19th century, even that was difficult for yacht racing.

In 1887, the club started from Southend one of the few non-stop round Britain races that has ever been held: there were eleven starters ranging from 40 to 255 tons, including the schooner *Aline*, owned by the then Prince of Wales (later owner of *Britannia*). In 1893 occurred one of classic races of yachting history on a round the buoys course organized by the club, when the season was opened off Gravesend by the 'big class', four huge cutters (each about 125ft, 38m), *Britannia* (the Prince), *Valkyrie II*, *Calluna* and *Ivernia*. *Britannia*'s win in perfect spring conditions was the beginning of many years for the royal cutter (later owned by King George V) and the aping of her design, which had been radical on her launch.

Between the world wars, the club was part of the big regatta season which wound its way round the coasts of England. So the season would start with a regatta off Southend, followed by a mid-summer course in the Solent and then races from Ryde Pier (to the east of Cowes, Isle of Wight) in the week before Cowes Week.

Since 1911 the club had a house at 80 Piccadilly, but in 1923 it moved to palatial headquarters at 60 Knightsbridge, known at that time as Hyde Park House. The old five storey building had huge assembly rooms. An immense 'smoking room' was never entered by ladies, except at the annual club ball. In 1961, the whole building was torn down; two and a half years later, the present club was occupied, the value of the site enhanced by eight storeys, above and slightly back from the club, sold off.

In 1955, a syndicate of the club built a new IYRU 6-metre, *Royal Thames*, and in it won the One Ton Cup. In the early 1970s, it began its present practice of running major international and national events: these have included the Soling Worlds, in 1970, the Half Ton Cup in 1971 and the Quarter Ton Cup in 1973. In 1975, the club had a series of major events for its bicentenary year. There was a commemoration service for the founder, the Duke of Cumberland, a transatlantic race (12 starters) from Newport, RI, to the Solent and an immense review in the Solent with lines of yachts inspected by both the Prince of Wales and Earl Mountbatten (assassinated four years later in Ireland). There was a bicentenary regatta at Cowes and a dinner in the Guildhall in London. Writing nearly twenty years later, one wonders whether such (harmless) excess would ever be repeated for a yacht club.

Classes

There are no regular classes, but the club frequently manages the championships of national and other classes, at various locations. Until the demise of the IOR level rating classes, it held regular 'nationals' for them and sometimes ran international regattas when they were allocated to Britain. Typical regattas are those run for the IYRU 6-metre class, Sigma 38, Sigma 33, International Etchells 22 and International J 24.

One of the largest size of offshore one-designs was initiated by the club, when the then Rear Commodore, David Diehl, called a meeting there. It was created as the 'inter-club one-design' and became the Sigma 38 (it is now run by its own class association). In 1964, the club challenged for the *America's* Cup with the 12-metre, *Sovereign*. In 1974, it ran the challenger elimination trials at Newport, RI.

Hundreds of historic half-hull models in the comfortable Knightsbridge rooms of the Royal Thames Yacht Club.

Events and regattas

Many classes and local clubs have cause to thank the Royal Thames for its support in arriving at a coastal location with its race team and boats. Some of the classes which have benefited are mentioned above. There is approximately equal weight given to racing, cruising and social activity. There are three cruising rallies each year, two in British or French waters and one further away, for instance Turkey. There is a cruising cup for the best log.

There are functions in London including lectures, cocktail parties, theatre visits and formal dinners. Amongst the latter are annual prize-giving , ex-flag officers and senior member occasions.

Members

1,470 : Patron, HRH Prince Philip; Admiral, HRH The Prince of Wales; Commodore, HRH The Duke of York. There are 14 members of royal families including those of Belgium, Denmark, Holland, Greece, Norway, Spain, Sweden.

Address

60 Knightsbridge, London, SW1X 7LF, England.
℡ 071 235 2121

Royal Hawaiian Ocean Racing Club

This organization emphasizes how a yacht club can well be formed to fulfil a specific purpose. Some of the challenging clubs for the *America*'s Cup are in this category; so was the Royal Ocean Racing Club in England (page 71), created without a clubhouse in order to run a 600-mile race every year. The Royal Hawaiian Ocean Racing Club, with no member facilities of its own is a tax exempt organization under US law for the purpose of conducting the Hawaiian International Ocean Racing Series, currently for, and known as, The Kenwood Cup.

'The royal' is self styled, but is inherited from the old royal family of Hawaii which ruled the islands until 1893 (by which time many yacht clubs around the world were in existence. Hawaii was annexed by the USA in 1900 and is now, with its seven inhabited islands, a state of the union.) The crown of King Kalakaua is in the burgee over a native canoe.

Clubhouse
There is no house, but permanent race headquarters is in a two storey building shared with the Trans Pacific Yacht Club and has administrative, technical, computer and communications arrangements. It is in the Ala Wai Boat Harbor in the Waikiki part of Honolulu. There is a full time Executive Director and other staff.

History
The club was formed on 26th April 1985, when what was then called the Clipper Cup, presented by the then air line *PanAm*, had been running annually in one form of offshore event or another since 1972. The regular race had been the Around the State Race, which involved 775 miles encircling the islands. Its entries began to fall off after about five years and so the Clipper Cup was presented to include a series of inshore races as well as the long event. The Waikiki Yacht Club ran this until 1985. In 1990, the Around the State was dropped in favour of a 390 mile Kaula Race and an ocean triangle. In 1986, the Kenwood Corporation of Japan became responsible for the sponsorship.

Countries whose boats have participated in the international series are Australia, Brazil, Bermuda, Britain, Brunei, Canada, France, Hong Kong, Italy, Japan, New Zealand, Philippines, Russia, South Africa, Switzerland, Thailand, and the USA.

Classes
In the series only ocean racing yachts take part, rated to the international rules, IMS and IOR.

Events and regattas
The series is each even year, 1990, 1992, 1994. The Waikiki Yacht Club remains a joint organizer (though all work is handled by the RHORC; the burgees of the Hawaii Yacht Club and the Kaula Yacht Club are also acknowledged. In recent years the number of entries has been in the high 40s (in 1982 it reached 80, all IOR). The present format, open to yachts over 35ft (10.7m) LOA, is four ocean triangles of about 24 miles, one medium distance of 150 miles and the 352-mile long race. This is from Honolulu around Kaula, Niihau, Kauai and return. The entry fee is currently $500 and $1,000 for yachts with advertising. The trade wind invariably blows, Hawaii being in the tropics at latitude 21 degrees 19 minutes north.

Members

Open to those who have completed the Kenwood Cup series, or 600 miles of other ocean races. General membership meeting during the series, when ten directors are elected for the next two years.

Address

Ala Wai Boat Harbor, 1739 C-1 Ala Moana Blvd., Honolulu, Hawaii 96815, USA.
✆ 808 946 9061

Competitors of international level relax at the Hawaii Yacht Club during the Kenwood Cup series.

The Kenwood Cup.

Royal Hong Kong Yacht Club

This thriving club in the crown colony of Hong Kong, one of the wealthiest territories in the world, is more active than ever after nearly 150 years. It must be one of the few clubs in the world which now needs a rule stating *'private servants are not allowed on club premises'*. There are three club stations and ample sailing waters. As will be read below, the running of this club is a big operation, possibly even the most extensive that exists outside the USA. The club has frequently represented the colony in major offshore series such as the Admiral's Cup and Southern Cross Trophy. The latitude is 22 degrees 18 minutes north.

Clubhouses
There are three club stations, but the main complex is on Kellett Island. It was originally the naval powder magazine given to the Royal Hong Kong Yacht Club in 1937 in exchange for a previous club site at North Point required by the government.

In addition to all the usual club rooms such as main bar, cocktail bar, restaurant, library (book and video) offices and verandah, there are a coffee shop, bowling alley, squash courts, swimming pool and exercise room. Adjoining are a boatyard, workshop, training base, hardstanding, car park and 'Activities Ahoy!' The club runs a bus service from Central to Kowloon and a boat service from Kowloon to Kellett Island.

The clubhouse on Middle Island is for rowing and dinghy sailing. The club has rowing boats there and fleets of Wanderer and Optimist sailing dinghies. Shelter Cove station has a marina as a base for cruising boats. Barbecues and simple meals are available at the clubhouse.

To run all these facilities there is a considerable permanent staff with at least seventeen full time executives in charge of various departments. There are also numerous sub-committees and a dozen club class secretaries.

Waterside
There is a total of over 400 moorings in five locations. Boatyard attached to the club; day boats and dinghies are kept on hard standing ready for launching. Short stay berthing for visitors.

History
Two years before the *America*'s Cup was first raced at Cowes, the Victoria Regatta Club was formed and six cutter yachts sailed a race in Hong Kong harbour. That was in 1849, though there are records of the formation of a Canton Regatta Club which was for rowing in 1837 and a Hong Kong Regatta Club racing in the harbour in 1845. A Hong Kong Corinthian Sailing Club appeared to exist in time to fuse with the Canton club in 1893. Application was then made to the Admiralty to become the Royal Hong Kong Yacht Club and have the use of a blue ensign, defaced by dragon and crown.

In 1908 the club moved from the Naval Coalyard in Kowloon to a new clubhouse built at North Point (see above). In 1933 a naval volunteer reserve was formed from members of the club. In 1941 Hong Kong was captured by the Japanese. On the 17th September 1945, HMS *Vengeance* stood off Kellett Island and her officers re-opened the club. Since then it has mirrored the expansion of racing and dinghy sailing around the rest of the world,

A sumptuous establishment: the Royal Hong Kong Yacht Club.

British practices, customs and classes being followed and, of course, improved upon. The club has established probably more reciprocal arrangements (page 11) with other clubs than any other: in the UK 20 including 16 royal clubs; in Canada and USA 33 including 6 royal; in Australia and New Zealand 13 including 8 royal; Far East 11 including 3 royal; continental Europe 8 including 6 royal; elsewhere (Indian Ocean, Gulf) 6 including 2 royal. (This is given in full, as it shows a remarkable network of yacht clubs and says something about their status).

Classes
Impala, Sonata, Ruffian 23, Pandora, International Etchells 22, International Dragon, International Flying Fifteen, L class, Laser, Wanderer, Optimist. X-99, ocean racer, cruiser-racer (using Channel Handicap System, IMS and Portsmouth Yardstick)

Events and regattas
Apart from sailing, regular club activities include children's swimming lessons, Chinese painting, chess club, mothers and babies swimming, aerobics, squash contests.

The main races are the China Sea Race and the Hong Kong to San Fernando, Philippines, on alternate years, the China Coast Race, Round the Island Race, spring and autumn regattas, two annual races to Macau. The main season is from September to the end of May. The summer months are very hot and there is a danger of typhoons. July and August are the quietest months. During the season all classes have regular weekend racing for various trophies and grouped series; however a typical Saturday might have eleven classes racing.

Major social events include annual grand ball, prize givings, Bluff Island barbecue, Christmas, Boxing Day and new year parties, Burns Night supper, St Patrick's Day party.

Members
3,675 resident; 4,281 'absent'; total 7,956. Patron: HM The Queen; Vice patron: HE The Governor of Hong Kong.

Address
Kellett Island, Causeway Bay, Hong Kong.
℡ 852 832 2817

The magnificent emblem
of the Royal Hong Kong YC.

Multihull or multi boats, it is always busy at Grafham Water.

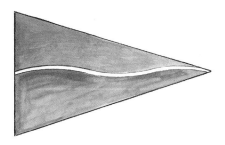

Grafham Water Sailing Club

Many of the waters round the British Isles can be inhospitable for sailing at any time of year, the chief reasons being swiftly changing weather and strong tidal streams; there is therefore considerable attraction in usable stretches for inland sailing. The result: no current and a weather shore somewhere. Grafham Water, sixty miles north of the centre of London, is three miles long and one mile across, giving 1,600 acres free for sailing. The surrounding countryside of Cambridgeshire is essentially flat, typical of the east side of England. This makes the wind steady and also available in light conditions. From the clubhouse, in about a mid-point along one shore, all racing courses can be seen, which adds to general safety.

Clubhouse
The building is a multi-storey block designed specifically for its task. The ground floor consists of bar and restaurant. The first floor, above it, has the changing rooms and showers. The second floor has the club offices and a top deck bar with views across the Water. It is often used for special functions or for hiring to members. The race starting box is alongside the club, as is a children's play area.

Waterside
There are 16 cruiser spaces and more than 800 dinghy and keel-boat spaces with direct launching from 5 slipways at all times.

History
In 1966 the Diddington Valley was flooded to create a reservoir. The Great Ouse Water authority which had the responsibility for Grafham Water after building the 5,600ft dam at one end, gave permission for a sailing club to operate. In June 1966, the club was opened by HRH Prince Philip. From the earliest days, the Water has been used for Olympic indicator trials.

Classes
Enterprise, Fireball, 505, Flying Fifteen, Laser, Wayfarer. Catamarans, Hurricane, Dart and handicap, handicap dinghies (Portsmouth Yardstick), sailboards. Keel-boats and special classes at nominated regattas and trials.

Events and regattas
There are more than a dozen marks anchored around the Water. The club is open seven days per week all the year round. The fixtures are extensive with a plan for club and visiting classes on all weekends and days mid-week. Annual occasions include Grafham Grand Prix (nearest Sunday to 1st January), Duke of Edinburgh Trophy which is the clubs main regatta, charity race for Royal National Lifeboat Institution.

There are sound rules on safety including special clothing in the winter, no landing around the reservoir, a restricted area for sailboards and a highly trained rescue boat organization. Gentle cruising is encouraged and there is training to national authority standards.

Members
1,800 : The subscriptions are remarkably low though there are boat fees. As a 'user club' there is currently no waiting list.

Address
Perry, Huntingdon, Cambridgeshire, PE18 0BU, England. ✆ 0480 810478

Royal Brunei Yacht Club

Brunei, small in area (an irregular 60 by 50 miles), is famed for its wealth and particularly that of its ruler the Sultan. Surrounded by the federation of Malaysia, it opted for independence when the British relinquished the protectorate, which had been held since 1888 until the Japanese occupation in 1941. In June 1945, Brunei was liberated by the Ninth Australian Division; in the decades which followed oil brought prosperity and many British expatriates to the country. In the early 50s, one or two (heavy) Snipe racing dinghies appeared, probably from clubs in Hong Kong or Singapore and on the 29th September 1952 a handful of expatriates and Bruneians formed themselves into a yacht club. Almost immediately it became the Royal Brunei, the 'royal' derived from the Sultanate and not from the British crown (so no Admiralty warrant in this case was needed nor sought). The deeply indented Bay of Brunei is well into the tropics at 5° north.

Clubhouse
There are two spacious, cool clubhouses. One is at Kota Batu and was once the house of a member; it opened in 1986. The other is the Serasa clubhouse, built on a man made spit near Badukang Island. Originally quite small, it has been extended in 1983 and 1985. 'A good place for families despite the sand-flies and the litter left on the beach by the tide'. A swimming pool is under construction. There is berthing for short stay near the former and dinghy launching at both club sites.

History
The Brunei law required notification of the formation of any club or society and this was done. The club began by meeting on a disused fishing boat, *Tenggiri*, but HRH the Sultan suggested the use of a factory manager's vacated residence at Subok. By 1954, the club had seven Snipes and about fifty members, who used them by ballot. The social life of the club was inextricably mixed with the expatriate life in Brunei and with two other clubs emerging in the country, there were interclub events. In 1959 Brunei became fully responsible for its own internal affairs. The members from then on tended to be government officers, police and hospital staff, mostly British, but also Australian, Indian and South African. Unlike clubs in the home countries, the colonial culture meant that it was positively used for business meetings and functions.

In December 1962 there was a rebellion in Brunei which was quickly suppressed when British Marines arrived, though not without casualties. The arrival of British troops in some numbers resulted in a number of officers becoming members of the club, one later becoming commodore. This club must be the only one to field a regular rugby football team, not to mention yacht club cricket and darts sections.

The Snipes were sailed for many years, but the Hornet class was slowly introduced in the 60s. The last Snipe was ceremoniously burned in 1987, by which time there were also GP 14s. After them came the Lazy E class, but these had been built in England using resin glue unsuitable for the tropics and they all had to be virtually rebuilt. By 1975, club membership was 400 and by 1979 a limit of 600 was put on it, with a waiting list (later it has become 800 and growing). All this was due to the growth of prosperity caused by the oil and gas finds. In 1974, the Lazy Es were replaced by a mixture of 470 and Javelin class racing dinghies. In 1985 it became compulsory to wear a buoyancy aid when racing, though some sailors still dislike this requirement in the hot climate.

Later classes to arrive in the club were in 1982 the Laser 2, the Fireball and the Hobie 16 catamaran. In these years the local fixture list grew out of all recognition, as did a range of team and inter club races against clubs in such places as Hong Kong and Singapore.

Classes
Fireball, Javelin, Hobie 16, Laser 2.

Events and regattas
Season runs from May to January, avoiding the monsoon. Annual HM Sultan's Trophy, Dairy Farm Plate, Queen's Birthday Regatta, Commodore Trophy, Long Distance race, Trafalgar Trophy, Open series and others. Midsummer Ball, Laying up dinner, Christmas and new year parties.

Members
800.

Address
PO Box 272, Bandar Seri Begawan 1902, Negara Brunei, Darussalam.
℄ 673 2 786139

The KDY club branch at Rungsted in winter weather.

Kongelig Dansk Yachtklub

Each of the Scandinavian kingdoms has a senior club invoking the name of the nation, which in earlier days was also the national authority for sailing (see the history of the Yacht Club de France, p 39). The English translations are simply the Royal Norwegian Yacht Club, the Royal Swedish Yacht Club and the Royal Danish Yacht Club. Despite the growth of many other sailing and yacht clubs in all three countries, the Kongelig Dansk Yachtklub, in the case of Denmark, remains prominent with all leading sailors as members, as well as of their local club. Major regattas in the country are invariably under its burgee. However the largest yacht racing start ever recorded in the world, which is the Danish Round Zeeland Race (Sjaelland Runt) happens to be organized by another club, the Helsingør Amateur Sailing Club. On 21st June 1984 a record 2,072 yachts started.

There are two countries in the world which are widely considered as 'sailing mad': one is New Zealand (p 154) and the other is Denmark.

Clubhouse
For more than 100 years, the main clubhouse has been the Langelinie-Pavillonen on the waterfront of the capital city, Copenhagen. It lies in a park in view of the famous statue of the Little Mermaid. The present building was completed in 1960. The club offices are here and a restaurant is open for lunch on weekdays. For weekend and summer sailing and the berthing of yachts, the Skovshoved clubhouse is used which lies to the north of the city and port. It is open from May to September; there is a marina here for 350 yachts with boatyard and fuelling. A third facility for members (note the large number

below) since 1980 is a clubhouse owned jointly by KDY and Rungsted Kyst Yachtklub, adjoining a 750 berth marina. Rungsted is eleven miles up the coast towards Helsingør (Elsinore). It also is closed in the winter, which may be hard and ice riven, unless reserved for a private function.

Waterside
From the marinas at the clubhouses mentioned above, members can sail their boats straight out into the relatively sheltered tideless waters of the western Baltic with the Danish islands south and west, the Swedish coast to the north and, in recent years, the whole coast of Germany, no longer forbidden. Yachting ports and marinas are very numerous.

History
Although formed thirty-six years after the Kungelig Svenska (Swedish) Sallskapet in 1866 (Denmark was not a fully independent country before that), the initial twenty-eight members were able to hold two regattas that year. The original name was simply the Danish Yacht Club, but membership and numbers of yachts and starts increased over the years. For instance in 1880 there were 400 members and 77 starts; in 1885 there were 900 members and 94 starts. In 1891 King Christian IX granted the royal title to the club. In 1884, the first proper clubhouse was built at Langeline, a pavilion-like edifice of turrets and verandahs. It lasted until 1902, when an altogether more substantial building was constructed closer to the water, where keel-boats were moored and a small boat pier was available. Unfortunately it was used by

the German navy during the occupation and totally destroyed by precision bombing in 1944. After that the club had temporary accommodation on the site until the present fine clubhouse was ready in 1960. Meanwhile the members had moved out in 1941 to begin the Skovshoved base.

Denmark took a leading part in the rationalization of racing and rating rules at the beginning of this century. When the IYRU was founded at conferences of the countries of Europe in London (1906 on the rating rule) and Paris (1907 on the racing rules), the KDY represented the country and major influence was wielded by Alfred Benzon, one of the only four ordinary members of the permanent committee. The others were a Frenchman, a German and two Englishmen. The chairman and secretary were also British (it was explained at the time that the tonnage of British and colonial yachts was equal to twice that of the other eleven member countries of the IYRU combined).

Thereafter Denmark, as well as Norway and Sweden, was a major protagonist in the international (metre) racing classes. The club achieved 1,000 members in 1905. Royal patronage was always close, but particularly in the reign of King Christian X who sailed regularly until the end of his reign in 1947 from Skovsoved, even during the years of World War II.

In 1948, Paul Elvstrom won the single-handed dinghy class at the Olympics in Torbay, England. This was the first of four consecutive gold Olympic medals, breaking all kinds of records for all sports. His success and the whole racing cult around this sailor has had much to do with the people of Denmark being 'sailing mad'. In 1966 the KDY held a particularly widely acclaimed jubilee year. With less competing events than we have thirty years later, all kinds of races from European countries, a transatlantic race world championships for numerous classes were organized by KDY.

Once again when major international rule making was in progress KDY, in the form by now of the Dansk Sejlunion, took a leading part. This was the creation of the IOR (International Offshore Rule for ocean racing) in the years leading up to 1969. A series of meetings were held at the club, which united the American, British and other safety and equipment regulations.

Classes
Cruiser-racer, offshore racer (IMS and DH (Danish Handicap)). International Dragon, all Olympic classes, Hobie 16.

Events and regattas
The annual Skaw Race is jointly run by KDY and clubs in Norway and Denmark, whatever the exact course of 350 miles, it always rounds the Skagen light on the northern tip of Denmark. Combined offshore races in Danish, German and Swedish waters. Two or three major class championships per year. Cruising rallies; the Baltic Sea Cup for the best extended cruise in the Baltic. Many functions in the clubhouses, including KDY spring ball.

Members
2,400 : Patron: HM The Queen of Denmark. Each member receives the magazine *Sejlsport* six times per year.

Address
Langelinie-Pavillonen, 2100 Kobenhavn 1, Denmark
℡ 45 3314 8787

The KDY shield in oak, preserved from the earliest club house at Langelinie.

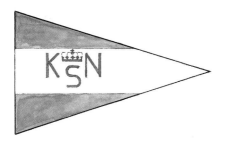

Kongelig Norsk Seilforening

The Royal Norwegian Yacht Club is a sure centre for all Norwegian yacht racing and sailing. The royal family has been very active in the front rank of competitive sailing for many years and like the other Scandinavian countries, Norway is a land of seafarers. Its very long and beautiful coastline is a cruising challenge, which stretches as far as the arctic circle. However the club and its activities are more likely to be found in the Skagerrak and approaches to Oslo.

Clubhouse
The clubhouse is in the capital city of Oslo, on the waterfront. There is an adjoining marina of 550 berths with cranes up to 2 and 10 tons respectively. Dinghy launching and visitors' berths are available.

History
The club was founded in 1883 while Norway was in the process of becoming a separate nation from Sweden. It had its own king only from 1905. Members of the KNS were immediately enthusiastic about racing boats to the International (metre) Rule created in 1907. They scored a run of successes when these metre boats were the basis of the yachting Olympic Games. In 1920, they won the 8-metre class; 1920, 6s, 8s, 10s and 12s; 1924 6s and 8s; 1928, 6s. This latter 6-metre was skippered by Crown Prince (later King) Olav. In the 1952 Olympics, which were in the Baltic (Helsinki), Norway won the Dragon class and was second in the 5.5-metre and 6-metre.

For many years King Olav was a senior officer of the IYRU (International Yacht Racing Union) and was instrumental in preserving the racing of keel-boats built to the International rule in the face of pressure around the world from ocean racing boats and one-designs. The International One-Design (the only class to appropriate this name), a 'frozen 6-metre' originated in Norway in the late 30s and is still raced there.

The IOR One Tonner *Fram,* owned by Crown Prince (now King) Harald was very successful in the late 1980s. Now he is king, the government is reluctant to let him go offshore.

Classes
Cruiser-racer, offshore racer (DH, IMS, IOR, LYS (Scandicap); International 5.5-metre; 11m OD, First Class 8, H-Boat, International Soling.

Events and regattas
The annual Oslo to Ferder Race for all classes is in June and attracts about 1,000 starters. The club runs one or more international or continental championships each year. Much of the racing is based at Hankø further down the Oslo Fjord. This is a holiday island and an attractive rural yachting base with deep water, where often the royal yacht, *Norge,* can anchor, for the king to sail from or watch the racing. The Hankø Yacht Club, a small building but with a select membership, is there.

KNS joins with Danish and Swedish clubs to run the 350-mile Skaw Race, the main regular ocean race in the Kattegat.

Members
About 4,000 : Patron: HM King Harald V.

Address
Huk Aveny 1, 0287 Oslo, Norway.
✆ 47 2243 7410

South of Oslo, KNS uses Hankø.

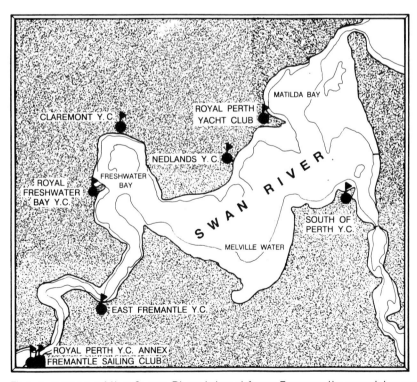

The expanse of the Swan River inland from Fremantle provides an
ideal area for racing. Numerous clubs are sited on the shores.

Royal Freshwater Bay Yacht Club

This is one of the leading clubs in the Perth and Swan River area of Western Australia. It is a place of major sailing waters in world terms. Elsewhere (pages 94 and 145) will be found details of the Royal Perth YC, winner and loser of the *America*'s Cup, and the Fremantle SC. This entry takes the opportunity of surveying other clubs in general. The Royal Freshwater Bay YC itself has a reputation as the most exclusive in the area and its members have 'old money'. It happens to be in a suburb where average age is high. Yacht crews in all races are obliged to wear blue and white dress, or individual yacht uniforms.

Clubhouse
This stands on a promontory with its own marina and in five and a half acres of landscaped gardens and lawns with a fine view over Freshwater Bay and Melville Water. There are bars, a restaurant and a function centre.

Waterside
The club itself has a marina with 280 berths, hard standing, slips and hoists. However the Swan River is actually a sizeable inland lake, so that all kinds of small boat sailing take place within it. To reach the Indian Ocean it is necessary to head seawards down a conventionally narrow part of the river, negotiating two bridges. Many yachts therefore have masts which can be lowered by their crews. Below the bridges the boats are in Fremantle, while a fishing boat harbour which was adapted in a major way for the *America*'s Cup (see Royal Perth YC Page 94) lies to the south of the river exit to the sea. The result of this configuration and the boat-mad Australians is one of the

greatest concentration of yacht clubs. There are thirty-one affiliated to the Yachting Association of Western Australia. It is not possible to give all their names, but a sample is Exmouth YC, Esperance Bay YC, Koombana Bay SC, Mounts Bay SC, Perth Dinghy SC, Rottnest Island YC, St George's Catamaran Club.

History
The club was founded in 1896 and granted the royal warrant in June 1934.

Classes
Cruiser-racer, offshore racer (IMS, IOR and YAH), International Dragon, Etchells 22, Flying 15, 505, 420, Mirror, Laser, Optimist. All sorts of classes are sailed in the Swan River from the many clubs.

Events and regattas
These include offshore racing series, 4 major races and a power yacht time trial. Cruising in company programme of 8 cruises including 14 day mid-summer cruise over Christmas. 30R series for older cruiser-racers of 30ft (9.1m). Regular series and championships for all classes. Overseas race teams in local keel-boats, for instance, visit to Cowes, England, for team races in the Daring class and return to Perth for the Colonial Challenge Cup in Etchells 22s.

Members
All categories, 1,690. Patron: His Excellency the Governor of Western Australia.

Address
Keane's Point, Peppermint Grove 6011, Western Australia.
✆ 010 61 9 384 9100

Oxford University Yacht Club

The two ancient universities of England have clubs and societies for every known activity. It is therefore no surprise that there exist the Cambridge University Cruising Club and the Oxford University Yacht Club. There is also described later the Oxford and Cambridge Sailing Society.

Clubhouse
The clubhouse was established in 1947 at Port Meadow, Medley, on the River Thames. It was in effect a building from a wartime airfield. In 1949, it was replaced with a larger structure where all the club boats could be stored and maintained. In other words it was more of a workshop than a conventional club. Since then facilities have been improved. The Thames, England's longest river has many miles to go the sea, as it wanders through the green valley close to Oxford city and university. At Port Meadow the river is wide enough for dinghy sailing.

Waterside
As well as Port Meadow, the OUYC has the use of the Oxford Sailing Club at Farnmoor Reservoir, about three miles from the centre of Oxford.

History
In the late nineteenth century there were sailed at Port Meadow, American style cat boats (heavy dinghies with a single big gaff sail supported by a mast well up in the bows). One had been shipped to England by the Marquis of Conyngham in 1852. This boat was widely copied at Cowes and in the Solent and a class also found it way to Oxford in the hands of private owners. In 1884, the Oxford University Sailing (as then called) Club was formed. It used similar boats at Port Meadow as well as one or two other sailing craft. Some of these boats were built by a local boatbuilder called Bossom; Bossoms Boatyard remained in business until present times and strangely was building wooden seagoing yachts at its Port Meadow yard. One undergraduate commissioned another local designers and builder called Smith to produce an unstayed mast yawl rigged, half decked sailing canoe in 1890 and others of the class followed.

Over at Cambridge the CUCC was formed in 1896 by some dons, but two years later undergraduates were also admitted. A match was then proposed between Oxford and Cambridge, but conditions could not be agreed. It was not until 1912 at Ely, near Cambridge, that a match was held. When the varsity match resumed in 1920, it was thereafter held at a neutral venue in borrowed boats.

In 1922, the OUSC held a major conference to decide on a suitable boat for racing. There were suggestions for a one-rater, half-rater, sharpie and various length sailing dinghies. The result was a new 14ft dinghy designed and built by Morgan Giles for the club's racing. The hulls were clinker with a single dipping lug sail with heavy centreboard and copper buoyancy tanks. Each time they tacked it was necessary to haul the heel of the yard to leeward of the solid wood mast. Yet the boats served the purpose of getting undergraduates racing: in 1926 an inter-college contest was started.

Another new design for club boats arrived in 1930. It was a 12ft dinghy, which Uffa Fox agreed to design for a fee of ten guineas (£10.50). It had a single Bermudan sail on a bamboo mast, but a jib was added in 1933. In 1931, the name was changed to the Oxford University Yacht Club, when the club absorbed a short-lived Oxford University Cruising Club.

In 1934, the Imperial Poona Yacht Club (page 101) was formed in an Oxford hotel and had close connections with the university. About this time the club applied for a 'half-blue' for sailing, but it was rejected on the grounds that it was not energetic enough (a 'blue' is a university award for distinction in a specific sport e.g. 'a rowing blue'). In 1936, the club purchased two of the new National 12 ft class of the standard Uffa King design made available by *Yachting World*. Proper one-designs at last took over in 1946, when the OUYC obtained six of the National Firefly 12 ft.

In a way the sequences of the OUYC can be said to represent the development of club dinghy sailing in England. From now on the club sent teams to race at home and abroad. Many different types of boat were used, depending on the venue.

For its own boats the club and CUCC moved to the 12ft Alpha in 1960, but this glass fibre dinghy with an inner and outer skin had inherent defects, as foam techniques for filling the gap between the skins, did not then exist. A major step in 1955 was the formation of the British Universities Sailing Association in order to send teams abroad from Britain, especially to the USA, where major tours have followed. In 1967, the university finally decided to give a full Blue for sailing. There were two for the Varsity match team and the remaining members of the team received half Blues.

The story of the ever changing club boat continued with the Lark replacing the Alpha in 1969 and being superseded in turn by the Laser 2 in 1980.

Classes
The club members sail various classes by invitation in matches against other universities or on arranged vacation regattas. The Laser II remains the club boat at Farnmoor; up-dated Firefly at Port Meadow.

Events and regattas
Annual competition within BUSA; Varsity match versus CUCC in six keel-boats in 'neutral' waters; Magnum internal team racing.

Summer garden party in Trinity term; winter dinner in Hilary term. Vacation tours with racing against opponents of foreign universities, for instance in Africa, Asia, France, Japan or the USA.

Members
100, also life members who give much support. As well as the usual three flag officers, there is a president and four vice-presidents, a captain of sailing and ladies captain.

Address
13 Berington Road, Oxford, OX2 6NB, England.

Port Meadow, Oxford, on the River Thames: home waters to the University Yacht Club.

Oxford and Cambridge Sailing Society

Many yacht and sailing clubs in the USA and UK are simply named after the institutions from which their membership is recruited. There are regiments, schools, commercial companies: Haberdasher' Aske's School SC, Household Division YC, US Coast Guard Academy SC. A list would be formidable. To have the names of two ancient institutions in the title must be very unusual. (The first Oxford college was founded in 1249; in Cambridge 1284). The Society is essentially for those who have left university and want to go on racing with those they met in the OUYC and the CUCC.

Clubhouse and waterside
None

History
The Oxford versus Cambridge sailing matches progressed (see previous), in a similar way to other inter university sports, such as the famous national occasions in rugby football and rowing eights ('the boat race'). As there was little team racing around England then, Stewart Morris and Roger de Quincy (famous racing sailors in their time), formed the society in 1934, so that the practised sailors could set up match racing in the season, long after they had 'gone down' from their universities. Why just Oxford and Cambridge? Well, there was always a strong social element and one wanted to enjoy an annual dinner with 'one's own sort of person'. Anyway to be eligible for membership, one had to have sailed in the Varsity match (i.e. Oxford versus Cambridge). The original membership was thirty and six more were permitted each year.

The seasonal routine was to challenge clubs, probably one which had one or two of its own members in it and sail in three one-design yachts per team. Members recalled that when at university, skippers were sometimes keener on shutting out a permanent rival from the home team, than sparring with the opposition.

Though the subscription was for more than fifty years kept at one guinea (£1.05), the funds enabled a supply of port to be purchased and laid down. As it takes twenty-one years to mature, the first bottles started becoming drinkable in 1944 and thereafter the annual dinner always had vintage port. Sad to say, by the 1980s team racing in general had passed through its popular stage and was becoming hard and with specialized techniques.

Classes
By invitation of host club

Events and regattas
Because of the 'professionalism' of team racing, there is now instead an Inter-generation team race each October at Farnmoor, Oxford (see OUYC); the older generation gets a handicap. Various matches, but in particular against Itchenor sailing Club and Wroxham Broad YC for 1992 memorial models to Stewart Morris, founder. Annual dinner in March, usually at Royal Thames YC (page 109); annual cocktail party in London, early December.

Members
225. No flag officers: there is a president and committee.
HM King Harald of Norway is a member.

Address
Secretary, c/o Thorn Villa, Thorn Way, Long Itchington, Rugby, Warwickshire CV23 8PF.
℡ 0926 814921

Island Sailing Club

This modest name conceals the cult of 'the Island'. It is the club where sailors gather in large numbers during major events at the racing port of Cowes. There are six major old established clubs in Cowes, all within a couple of minutes walk of each other (it is difficult to think of anywhere else with such a concentration). The annual event where this is most marked is the Round the Island, which in 1989 attracted 1,781 starters.

Clubhouse
This is right on the Cowes waterfront with one of the world's most magnificent views of yachting. It was built in 1957 on the site of two previous clubhouses. On the first floor is a large bar/lounge/dining room and balcony running the full length. This the main vibrant social area. On the ground floor are the administration, changing rooms and boat stores. On a second floor are the roof terrace, centenary room, which can be privately booked, small members-only bar and race control. Races can be started direct from the club by transit or from its flag pole to an outer distance mark in Cowes Road.

Waterside
Floating pontoon (dock) on the end of a long jetty. Members can bring their yachts alongside at most tides, but more often it is used for embarking on the club launches to join yachts on moorings in Cowes harbour, particularly racing keel-boats. Dinghies on concrete apron and slipway suitable for small keel-boats and dinghies. Landing though is the essential facility as the club is both in the town and on the water. There are big marinas nearby and facilities for yachts of world class.

History
In 1889 there were two clubs in Cowes, the Royal Yacht Squadron and the Royal London Yacht Club, but these did not provide racing for the small raters and one designs. As a result the club was formed by local men under its name which has remained unchanged. Unusually, women were admitted at an early stage. Purposely it has neither sought, nor been offered a 'royal' title nor special ensign. The first secretary (unpaid) was an architect; he designed and had built the first clubhouse, on the present site, for £300. The slipway for the use of members was appreciated, as the public slipways were insecure. The original subscription was one guinea (£1.05 or $1.50) and this remained the same for fifty years.

In the 1920s the club joined with others to create a 14 ft dinghy class. This was of rugged clinker design. In the 1950s, the island scow, a 10ft single sailed dinghy was raced. Meanwhile members were racing whatever were the current keel-boats in Cowes, now as listed below. In 1947, the club presented as a wedding present to the heir to the throne HRH Princess Elizabeth and her husband, Prince Philip, a Dragon class yacht, *Bluebottle*. Later Cowes town gave Prince Philip a Flying Fifteen class *Coweslip* (the latter now retired is preserved in Cowes Maritime Museum). These gifts restored the royal connection with active Cowes racing which had ended with the death of King George V in 1936.

The Round The Island Race, a midsummer event for 'cruisers' (and ocean racers and keel-boats) which starts in the early morning from Cowes and ends there in the evening after sailing the 49.65 nautical miles westabout around the Isle of Wight was first held in 1931. That attracted twenty-five starters.

By 1939 it was sixty; 1949, 100; 1960, over 200; 1963, over 300; 1969, over 400; 1974, over 500. The numbers passed 500 in 1981, then soared to the record 1,781 in the 1989 race. After that there was a slight but steady decline. Writing in 1994, it may be holding at around 1,200. (The world's biggest number of starters was 2,072 on the Round Zeeland Race in Denmark in 1984: it subsequently declined to about 1,100 each year).

Events and regattas
In addition to the annual Round The Island, there are other passage races of which the Nab Tower event is popular. There are weekends for keel-boat classes co-ordinated with other Cowes clubs. The club runs one of the days in the annual Cowes Week Regatta.

In the season there is racing every Tuesday evening. Intense lecture and social programme, especially in the winter for Island members.

Classes
Cruiser-racers (CHS, local handicaps), Dragon, E22, Flying Fifteen, Wight Scow, J-24. National championships run for various classes almost each year.

Members
2,600. Patron HM The Queen. Many leading British sailors are members, as they probably race in something at Cowes each year, also members of the royal family. However no membership list is ever published.

Address
High Street, Cowes, Isle of Wight PO31 7RE, England
℡ 0983 296621

This view of the ISC clubhouse will be familiar to anyone who has sailed into Cowes. It is justifiably popular with all types of yachtsmen from international racing crews to local cruising yachtsmen.

Royal Northumberland Yacht Club

The north-east coast of England has been primarily a scene of heavy industry for two hundred years and hardly a yacht cruising ground. Coal is actually washed up on beaches from underwater seams and is still collected by some inhabitants. This long established club shows the depth of enthusiasm for sailing in England; where there is salt or fresh water, then may be found a sailing club. Traditionally the port of Blyth was for the shipment of coal and pits can be seen just inland from the harbour. The club is cleverly housed afloat in a sheltered part of the port and yachts moor immediately off it. Among many other facets for which the club is well known, its name has been for many years on the only standard yacht pilotage book for the nearby coastline, *The Royal Northumberland Yacht Club Sailing Directions for the North-East Coast of England.*

Clubhouse

This substantial, wooden (teak on oak), dry and comfortable ship is an admirable clubhouse, so members are afloat even when not out in their boats! It is called H/Y (house yacht) *Tyne III* and was first fitted out for use of the club in 1954, though it has been continually improved and, of course, surveyed from time to time. It had previously been a lightship stationed at Calshot Spit, far away south in the Solent. The previous club ship had capsized at her moorings in a northerly gale in 1949: the steward and his wife were sleeping aboard and managed to get ashore in the middle of the night with no possessions just before the vessel turned over.

The club had used a ship as its headquarters since 1899 and there had been two earlier vessels moored in Blyth: coal dust until recent years was a drawback! During both world wars the respective house yachts were requisitioned; in 1939-1945, it was used as a ward room and mess for female personnel from the operations rooms of the submarine base in Blyth.

Waterside

Obviously this is right alongside the house yacht, that part of the harbour being given over to yachts. Blyth harbour is of the artificial variety with a channel entered between breakwaters and piers. The prevailing wind is offshore all along this coast, which alleviates the potential bleakness of it. However easterly gales can cause seas to break across the entrance of the port. Visiting yachts are assured of a berth in 'south harbour', where the club is moored.

History

The Northumberland Sailing Club was founded for sailing at the small port of Alnmouth in 1890 and in the custom of the day, the club met in a city, Newcastle-upon-Tyne. Again typically the first president was the Duke of Northumberland. However unlike most of the early English clubs, where social conventions in this respect have changed, his successors have ever since held the post. The then Duke presented '*a very fine*' Challenge Cup in 1897; the present Duke, in 1990, the club centenary year, also presented a trophy.

At about the turn of the century, the boats moved to Blyth harbour and the house yacht tradition began. In the first part of the twentieth century, Viscount Runciman and

Back in the 60s, boats crowding around the Royal Northumberland Yacht Club's floating clubhouse.

his family were active senior members of the club, as well as sailing in other parts of England, more fashionable for racing. They assisted in obtaining the title 'royal' and the new name, RNYC, dated from 1935. About this time there was a class of 'Seabirds', of which few details are available. There was a tendency to buy up racing yachts which English south coast sailors considered were outclassed and at one stage there were half a dozen 6-metre yachts. In the 50s and 60s, dinghy racing took hold and there was regular racing for one hundred Ospreys, Merlin Rockets, GP14s (two-thirds of the total) and Cadets. In contrast to today, it is interesting that all these were British classes, although the Cadet alone was also officially international.

Classes
Cruiser-racers on time allowance (NECRA, see below).

Events and regattas
The efficiency and seaworthiness of modern offshore racers changed the face of racing on this relatively exposed coast. In the thirties small yachts chose their weather and cruised along the coast, but by the late 50s onwards, there were many passages to Scandinavia, Holland and the Baltic. In 1965 was formed the North East Cruiser Racing Association by several clubs including the RNYC and today this is thriving with a series of ten or more offshore events every season. Many of these are up and down the coast, but there is a North Sea race to Ijmuiden, or other Dutch port. For many years and at the time of writing, NECRA has run its own rule of measurement and rating. The RNYC has its own regatta days in July or August which are open to NECRA boats. Racing dinghies are no longer catered for on a regular basis, as each class has developed its own special circuit. (Highways to tow dinghies by car and affluence, so that young people are crewing on ocean racers make the 60s seem an age away).

Sailing at the Royal Northumberland, a more regional club than some of the very famous names and not in an international racing centre, perhaps reflects the past and present of 'average' English yachting, after more than a hundred years continuity.

Members
785 : Patron: HRH Prince Philip. President: His Grace the Duke of Northumberland. Sir Walter Runciman, later Baron Runciman, then the Hon Leslie Runciman later Viscount Runciman were continuously commodore, then Admiral (1976) from 1931 until 1989, when the Viscount died; his heir was not interested in sailing.

Address
H/Y *Tyne III*, South Harbour, Blyth, Northumberland, England.
℡ 0670 353636

Coral Reef Yacht Club

The main sailing season in Biscayne Bay is a winter one, the peak being between Christmas and Easter; summer in south Florida is extremely hot. The club attracts residents of the huge Miami conurbation and people from other parts of the USA who have winter holidays or weekends in Florida. The sub-tropical climate means there is sailing all the year round. Not surprisingly the club is in demand for Olympic training and winter class championships.

Coral Reef YC was founded on 15th August 1955, having been formed five months previously as the 'Royal Palm YC'. There were sixty founder members, the first commodore being Edward S. Christiansen. Several years earlier there had been a 'South Florida YC', which had failed to prosper and Coral Reef YC also succeeded that.

Clubhouse
The site is in its own grounds , including car park, on the main road south from Miami to Coconut Grove, near the conurbation of Coral Gables; the area is heavily built up all along this coast. The building is large and stylish with swimming pool and club annexe. As in many American clubs, the public rooms are sizeable. There is a full restaurant service with ample staff, ballroom, wide lobby and club offices.

Waterside
The waterfront has been dredged out for docks to accommodate 200 yachts up to 45ft (13.7m) on marina berths. Adjoining are the Biscayne Bay and Coconut Grove Marina; near the club is a hauling out slip, so the whole appearance is of a large yacht harbour complex.

In 1992, one of the fiercest ever storms to hit Florida, Hurricane Andrew, cut a swathe through areas south of Miami. The club marina was wrecked and boats piled up on the shore. Part of the clubhouse complex was lost when the roofs were blown off, water levels came up over the shore and driving rain poured in. With characteristic enterprise and energy, the marina was completely rebuilt by spring 1993, while the clubhouse was operating with some temporary tentage and adopted buildings.

Classes
Star, J24, PHRF cruiser-racers. The Pelican and Pram are used for big junior training scheme, which as been established for many years.

Events and regattas
The club is a leading member of the Biscayne Bay YRA and events are numerous. Columbus Day Regatta musters 500 competitors. There are regular club cruiser races. Winter regattas for MORC (Midget Ocean Racing Club: offshore boats under 30ft (9.1m)) and Olympic classes. The Star class sails the annual Bacardi Cup course. In 1959 the club hosted the *Yachting* (magazine) One-of-a-Kind Regatta. This was a new concept which brought together one of each class of a category of boat, say, large centre-boarders and raced them to find comparisons. It was extended to cruisers and other types and copied abroad, especially in England. In recent years, pressure from the trade has watered down the results in favour of general comment. The early days were the best.

In the heyday of the SORC (Southern

Ocean Racing Conference), the club took a leading part running the Ocean Triangle (Miami – Great Isaac – Palm Beach – Government Cut); in 1958 and 1959, it had the greatest number of boats in the SORC, including that of *America*'s Cup winner Ted Turner, who for a time attracted attention to the club, with successes under its flag. In 1975, the club ran the World Three-Quarter Ton Cup. If it seems that these activities are mainly in the past, the club is an innovator and will no doubt continue to assist with new sailing ideas as they mature.

Members
900.

Address
2484 South Bayshore Drive, Coral Gables, Miami, Florida, USA.
✆ (305) 858 6303

The marina at the Coral Reef Yacht Club is for all year round sailing.

Antigua Yacht Club

Situated on the shore of the major Caribbean yachting port of Falmouth Harbour, which immediately adjoins English Harbour, on the island of Antigua, the Antigua Yacht Club combines the role of meeting place for visiting cruising and racing yachtsmen, marina headquarters and national authority for the nation of Antigua and Barbuda. It therefore has a seat on the IYRU. It also represents Antigua on the Caribbean Yachting Association (CYA), which has a number of functions including running the rule of measurement of rating (CYA rule) used widely in the region. The club was founded on the 21st November 1967 as the English Harbour Yacht Club. For three years club meetings and parties were held at the Admiral's Inn in Nelson's Dockyard.

Clubhouse
Dating from 1970, the clubhouse is combined with a large pub covering the ground floor and partly in the open in front of the club. The members' rooms and starting platform are on the first floor, but the club has the whole site on long lease. Showers and bathrooms adjoin the dinghy storage area. In the light of the transient nature of many visiting yachts and the wide varieties of crew, this has the admirable result of welcoming all in a paying area, while the permanent members have facilities for their own needs which overlook the anchorage and marina. At the time of writing G and T's Pizza has the pub and restaurant concession.

Waterside
Antigua Yacht Club Marina, which is managed separately, is a small but very useful berthing area. The main walkway runs straight out from the club and there are the usual fingers. Yachts also anchor stern – to the main pier, rise and fall of tide being negligible. There is electricity, water, ice, telephones, parking, taxi, car rental and cable TV.

However, there are other berths for yachts close by, anchoring immediately off, for example. Then there is a wide area for anchoring in Falmouth Harbour as a whole and another marina. English Harbour is immediately adjoining with the famous dockyard to which yachts can moor stern-to, or with numerous pleasant spots to anchor. From 1632 the harbour with the rest of Antigua was British, one of the few islands in the Caribbean never to have changed ownership until independence in 1981.

Classes
Racing dinghies including Laser; cruiser-racers to CYA rule.

Olympic classes train by moving around a Caribbean circuit.

Events and regattas
Races are open to all comers. Although sailing takes place all year round, the Hurricane season is July to October and the main season is December to the beginning of May. Each Thursday and on the last Sunday of every month, there is cruiser racing, especially for visitors, under CYA rating.

The main regattas of the year are at the end of each season in the last week of April and the beginning of May. There is the Classic Yacht Regatta and then the six day Antigua Sailing Week. 1992 was the twenty-fifth of these and it is one of the world's major

Lay-day during Antigua Race Week is based at the club.

regattas. Yachts are divided into numerous classes from 100ft (30.5m) ocean cruisers with power operated sails, through conventional ocean racers to production yachts of 35ft (10.7m). The entry list is invariably oversubscribed. Most yachts wear the flag of the UK with many from the USA and then groups from other European countries, Australia, Canada and nations from around the Caribbean.

The club supports the week, though a separate organization with a sponsor is formed to run it. Lay day is a major function for the club, when shoreside games are run in front of the clubhouse in the guaranteed tropical sunshine.

Members
800 : All the sailors resident in Antigua and waterside people.

Address
Falmouth Harbour, Antigua.
℡ 809 460 1799
(*Antigua Sailing Week*, PO Box 406, St John's, Antigua. ℡ 809 462 0036)

Royal Temple Yacht Club

There are clubs whose names simply reflect their localities such as Beer Sailing Club, in the village of that name on the south coast of England. Then there are those whose names appear to bear no relation to place, nor even to an institution such as the Household Division Yacht Club. One such is the Royal Temple YC. It is at the port of Ramsgate on the far south-east corner of England with the coast of France visible on clear days. The name originates in the heart of London on the River Thames, where were sited the Temple Steps, near to the Temple where chambers for barristers are to be found. The club originated with a group which used these steps as a customary place from which to sail. The Temple Yacht Club was founded in 1857; it became 'royal' the next year and moved out of London to Ramsgate in 1898.

Clubhouse

The clubhouse, built in 1890, looks over what is now the marina, the Downs (a famous old anchorage), the South Foreland and the Goodwin Sands. It is laid out in the old tradition with large dining room, well decorated bar and billiards room. The club has a number of magnificent trophies. There are eight bedrooms. It is open all year. Ramsgate is a compact and attractive town with a ferry terminal and the best yacht harbour on the English side of the Straits of Dover.

History

After the formation of the club, there was no clubhouse, but the members met in taverns near the Temple Steps, such as the Ship Tavern in Essex Street. (The street is still there, the pubs have various names!) The sailing races gradually moved down river away from the busiest built up area and docks. In 1860 a Mr William Antill was racing a 5-tonner called *Rifleman*: a painting remains in the clubhouse and the Antill Cup which the yacht won in 1868. By 1880 races were being run from Gravesend, which is well down stream of the Steps (which had really been deserted by now), to Ramsgate. As a result the present site was purchased and opened in May 1896.

In the great circuit around the coast of England in the early part of the century, the Royal Temple invariably gave an important regatta. It seems the club has always been remarkably active in the racing world: it challenged for the Coupe de France, brought it back to Ramsgate and defended it three times.

Classes

CHS (Channel Handicap System); Robber (ex-Quarter Ton).

Events and regattas

The club has an extremely busy programme. Cruisers are not forgotten, with a cruise to Holland and a three week cruise to Paris or some other continental destination, in a typical year. Cruiser-racers and offshore racers start with a spring series, then all summer there are numerous cross channel races to Boulogne and Calais, which are an afternoon sail.

Unlike some places, the starts and finishes for offshore yachts are immediately off the harbour. There are Saturday races and evening races. Major weeks are Offshore Race Week and the Round the Goodwins Race which is one of a series by east coast clubs run for the East Anglian Offshore Racing Association. Ramsgate Week in late August gets major support from members and visitors, including a number from nearby France, Belgium and Holland. Included in this is the Europa CHS team championship and the climax is the Ramsgate Gold Cup and the Victoria Cup, presented to the club by that queen.

The regatta committee places emphasis on family activities ashore and there are numerous amusements nearby plus a sandy beach either side of the harbour. The climate is frequently continental compared with other parts of the British Isles.

The R Temple YC is a prime example of a very ancient club, which has become one of the most modern in outlook. One reason is the clarity of its current aim which is '*the encouragement of amateur yachting.....embraces four functions: racing, cruising, navigation and sail training and social*'.

Members
802 : The oldest active member is said to be 90 years.

Address
6 Westcliff Mansions, Ramsgate, Kent, CT11 9HY, England.
✆ 0843 591766

Cups on offer in the Ramsgate Week regatta, including one presented to the club by Queen Victoria.

Ramsgate by night.

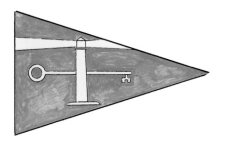

Key Biscayne Yacht Club

Key Biscayne is one of the many keys or string of islands on the south-east coast of Florida. Key Biscayne is joined by a causeway to Miami with the international airport less than twenty minutes from this club. Although uninhabited for many years, the Key now has many recent apartment blocks and a high proportion of retired people. Its anniversary handbook must be one of the few to mention both God and crematory in the opening pages. Social events; the tennis courts and sport fishing vessels play a major part in club activities. The club has a new float every year in the annual Fourth of July parade.

Clubhouse
This is a practical single-story building with a large restaurant, bar facing the water and meeting rooms. There are also spacious offices and stores. It is surrounded by a parking area, hardstanding for a number of medium sized yachts, dinghy park, swimming pool and verandah. A permanent security guard in his cabin is on the main gate. Adjoining land consists of residential streets and the church.

Waterside
As the club site is already sheltered by the lie of the land, it has only been necessary to lay out a single breakwater of 60,000 tons on one side. Three walkways with posts for bow or stern mooring accommodate some 90 boats right in front of the clubhouse. These were hit by a hurricane in 1965, when several boats sank.

History
The objects of the club stated in the charter are to promote boating, foster a spirit of helpfulness and good fellowship which will be a credit to 'our community' and to provide and maintain a location from which safe and economical boating can be enjoyed. The club was founded in 1955 and steps were taken to purchase a virgin site. The clubhouse and supporting area was then built from scratch, opening in 1958.

Events and regattas
The above quote from the charter shows that adventure is not really part of the philosophy at this convenient and smoothly run club. The commodore holds office for just one year so there have been many. However past commodores assemble in uniform and yachting caps for certain occasions. The main season, as in Florida generally, is in winter, but sailing and motor boating is possible all the year round. The summer is very hot.

Members
880 : As well as the usual flag officers, there is an appointment of SeaBelle Captain. This is the senior lady in the club each year, who, supported by a committee of SeaBelles, has a number of duties in the running of the club.

Address
180 Harbor Drive, Key Biscayne, Florida, 33149, USA.
305 361 9171

Key Biscayne YC clubhouse and marina in the sub-tropics of Florida.

The imposing old building of the Royal Irish Yacht Club.

Royal Irish Yacht Club

'In the 1820s and 1830s', said Douglas Phillips-Birt, the yachting historian, *'there were club creations which placed centres of yachting round the coast. Today some are like backwoods peers of an ancient aristocracy, links with that formative period of yachting'*. The Royal Irish Yacht Club was founded in 1831.

Clubhouse
The building, dating from 1848, must be one of the oldest yacht clubs to be still in use. What other ancient club is still in its original premises? Not the RYS which moved to its present site in 1856, nor the New York Yacht Club (1910). The clubhouse designed by John Skipton Mulvany (1813-1870), an *'architect of genius'*, is a classical building of distinction, conveying a sense of harmony and proportion. The interior layout has remained virtually unchanged for over 140 years. The entrance hall, symmetrical and welcoming, is lit by a domed skylight, which incorporates a symbolic compass rose.

History
Founded in 1831, the first commodore was the Marquess of Anglesey, well known as a leading member of the Royal Yacht Squadron; he commanded the cavalry at the Battle of Waterloo in 1815. The Duke of Wellington, (who vanquished Napoleon and was later prime minister of Great Britain) who of course was Irish, became a member in 1833 and Daniel O'Connell, the 'liberator', in 1846. Other members in their time were Sir Thomas Lipton (*America*'s Cup), George Birmingham (novelist), Conor O'Brien (pioneering ocean cruising man) and currently Robin Knox-Johnston.

Being in the harbour Dun Laoghaire of the capital, Dublin, it has played a leading part in the social and sailing progress of Ireland. Leading professional men tend to belong to the club which now includes lawyers, actors and writers. The club was host to the J24 world championship in 1990.

Waterside
The club has a fine view over the harbour and there are moorings for yachts there, including visitor moorings. Dinghies can be launched off a slip at the club.

Classes
International Dragon, Glen, Ruffian 23 International J24, cruiser-racers. Dinghies sailed, especially in a strong junior section are Laser, Laser 2, L'Equipe, Optimist.

Events and regattas
Annual regatta is the last Saturday in June each year.

Members
1,000 in various categories such as full, family and junior.

Address
Secretary, Royal Irish Yacht Club, Dun Laoghaire, Co. Dublin, Eire.
✆ 353 2809452

Howth Yacht Club

With the largest numerical membership of any club in Ireland, and a base in Howth harbour near Dublin, this active and long established organization and its relatively new clubhouse is within reach of a large segment of the country's population.

Clubhouse
In 1978 the harbour of Howth received major reconstruction. The club was able to acquire a previously unused site in the south-east corner of the port. An adjoining marina was constructed at the same time as the clubhouse and the whole arrangement was opened in July 1982. The club design had been selected through a competition run by the Royal Institute of Architects in Ireland. The club has all the amenities expected from a modern one including restaurant, bars, reading room, and billiard room. There are changing rooms and showers. It is an unusual design which symbolizes 'permanent regatta', the clubhouse and marina being integrated and employing a permanent staff of 24.

Waterside
Thus integrated, the marina has 220 berths and 24-hour security and there are also harbour moorings for members and visitors. A crane can lift up to 6.9 tons (7 tonnes). There is a dinghy park and launching slip.

History
The club has two parents. One is the Howth Sailing Club founded by forty-three original members in 1895; the other is Howth Motor Yacht Club which began in 1933. They were amalgamated in 1968. Many of today's members count their family links back to the earliest days including names like Guinness, Courtenay, Maguire, Hegarty and Lynch. The continuity of the sailing activities of these and others contributes to the club's distinct sense of community.

Like a certain number of clubs, a particular class has been part of the club story for years. Here it is the Howth 17, with length overall of 22ft 6in (6.9m) and original gaff rig designed by the club's first commodore, Herbert Boyd. The first races were in May 1898. The figure 17 refers to the waterline in feet. The class is the oldest one-design keel-boat still sailing in the British Isles and possibly, the world. Every inch a late Victorian cutter, there is a striking jackyard tops'l, often multi-coloured. The class strength of seventeen is maintained every season.

In 1983 a club member, John Gore-Grimes, became the first Irishman to win the famed Blue Water Medal of the Cruising Club of America. He sailed his standard Nicholson 31 to the Arctic, making passages such as Scoresby Sound, Greenland, southward, not previously undertaken by a yacht.

Classes
Howth 17, cruisers (including Shipman 28 and Folkboat), Puppeteer 22, National Squib, Laser, Mirror, Optimist.

Events and regattas
Weekend racing in all classes; Volvo autumn league each year; strong junior section with Laser 2 Regatta. Ocean racers from the club have represented Ireland in the Admiral's Cup (Cowes and Fastnet)

Members
1,880 : High entry fees and careful vetting of applicants.

Committee members have names like Brendan Connor, Seaumas O'Carroll, Dermot Skehan, Pat Murphy.

Address
Harbour Road, Howth, Co. Dublin, Eire.
℅ 010 353 1 322141

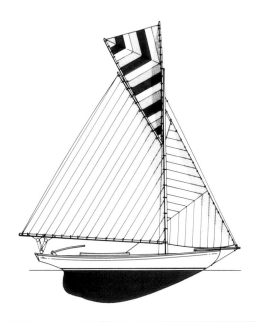

Howth YC is home of one of the world's most historic active classes, the Howth 17, first built in 1898.
It retains the jackyard topsail.

Howth Yacht Club and frontage.

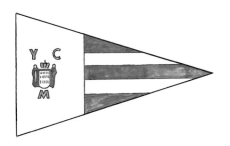

Yacht Club de Monaco

Monaco is essentially a country for the escapist and it has long been famous for international sport and leisure in many forms. In any photograph of the principality from the sea, it is the yachts, large ones both power and sail, that are conspicuous, moored as they are stern to the quays. Enclosed by France and not far from the Italian border, Monaco is nine miles from Nice and sixty miles by sea from Genoa with its yachting bases. The climate is northern Mediterranean.

Clubhouse
This is a substantial building at a seaward corner of the main harbour. The public rooms are large. The dining room is on the first storey with the standard of a top class restaurant. A large patio can be used for ceremonies and casual meals and drinks for visiting yachtsmen at moderate prices. Pictures and albums recount the maritime past of Monaco and its royal family.

Waterside
Thirty dinghies can be hauled out ashore permanently by the club. There are seventeen yacht berths for members and six short stay berths. The large harbour provides a haven for yachts of all sizes and for racing of dinghies and small classes. Once outside the port, cruising and racing is available all along the Riviera coast and the rest of the Mediterranean.

History
Founded in 1953, the club plunged straight in to the activities of modern sailing and boating. More than most of the clubs surveyed here, it has simply responded to the needs of yachtsmen without inhibitions. The membership has always been wealthy and the social life of Monte Carlo is unceasing. Royal patronage (by members of the family of the ruling prince) and participation in the sport was immediately built in. The Yacht Club de Monaco is the national authority represented in the IYRU.

Classes
Cruiser-racer, offshore racer (CHS, local handicaps). First Class 8, Surprise. International Star. Laser, Optimist.

Events and regattas
Season opens with Primo Cup for cruiser-racer one-designs and CHS in February. Other typical events in a season: Defi YC de France-YC de Monaco, Saint Jean championship for amateurs in many classes, J24 challenge with Manhattan YC of New York, Christmas – New Year Laser races. Offshore power boating with Monaco – Cannes – Monaco and Venice – Monte Carlo. Game Fishing meeting. Fully subscribed junior sailing programme all season. Children's AMADE Optimist Class Regatta in aid of Prince Albert clinic for children in Madagascar.

Members
1,000. Following the French system, the terms commodore etc and flag officer are not in use. A president and three vice-presidents. President: HSH (His Serene Highness) Le Prince Héréditaire Albert de Monaco.

Address
16 quai Antoine 1er, 98000 Monaco.
✆ 010 33 93 50 58 39

Monte Carlo harbour: busy centre for club and yachts.

Sailing from the Fremantle SC can either be in the Indian Ocean or in the spacious Swan River (top of picture).

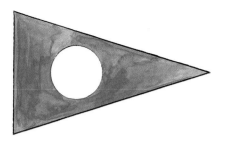

Fremantle Sailing Club

This is one of three major clubs close to Perth, Western Australia. It is an extremely active one. The others are the Royal Perth Yacht Club, long traditions and 'new money' and the Royal Freshwater Bay Yacht Club, the latter said to be somewhat exclusive ('old money'). There are some five further clubs. Fremantle and Swan River have for long been one of the world's most progressive sailing places, but in recent years they have been conspicuous owing to two very major international events: the *America*'s Cup (in 1986–1987) and the Whitbread Round The World Race (1990, 1994 etc).

Clubhouse
Built in 1979 right on the water, the two storey building has a large dining room which can take at times 400, bars and special function rooms on the first floor. There is an outside bar and space for barbecues. Club offices are in the main entrance and there is a separate ablution block. 640 car park spaces for members.

Waterside
A marina fronts the club with 720 yacht berths; in Australia the allocation of moorings of this kind is called 'penning'. Boat lifters, mast lifters, 30-ton crane, six all-weather launching ramps. There is a first week of free berthing for visitors.

History
Founded over one hundred years ago, the club's earliest activities were racing around the buoys in Cockburn Sound.

Classes
Ocean racer, cruiser-racer (IMS, IOR and JOG rating),
S&S 34, Adams 10, 470, 420, Mirror Dinghy.

Events and regattas
This club is one for multi-activity with inshore and offshore racing, dinghy sailing, angling and game fishing.

One reason for all this is that the climate enables such sport to continue all year round; latitude about 32° south. The heat causes a regular strong sea breeze, called 'the Fremantle Doctor'.

The calendar is packed, so it is hard to pick out one race or rally rather than another. Important events are the race to Bali, every third year; summer and winter inshore series every Saturday, ten offshore races annually, exact courses varying slightly. The Cruising Section has a regular programme of rallies and meetings. Junior and other training is in Laser, Mirror, 420 and 470 dinghies (the last is an Olympic class, so the club's standard of 'training' can be guessed at).

The club has been the host to the Whitbread Round The World Race stopover in 1989 and 1993, since the elimination of Cape Town from the route; this is a major effort much appreciated by the international competitors, though there has never been an Australian yacht in the Whitbread race.

Members
2,400 : For such numbers there are six flag officers and seven Captains, one for each activity. All office holders male. For such immense facilities and organization, members over 24 years pay about $A390 (£186). 1,400 boats based on the club.

Address
Marine Terrace, Fremantle, Western Australia 6160.
✆ 09 335 8800

1990s development for the Sandringham Yacht Club.

Start of the two-man marathon, Melbourne to Okinawa race.

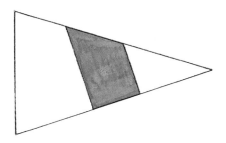

Sandringham Yacht Club

The club is one of a number in and around the large city of Melbourne, capital of the Australian state of Victoria. All look out on the land locked waters of Port Phillip Bay, some 725 square miles. The other clubs are the Royal Yacht Club of Victoria (founded 1853), the Royal Brighton YC (1875), the Royal Melbourne Yacht Squadron (1876), the Royal Geelong YC and Hobsons Bay YC. The yachting tradition is seen therefore to be very strong indeed. The yachting Olympic Games were held here in 1956, so far the only time the races have been in the southern hemisphere. This club is the largest in membership and boats in Port Phillip.

Clubhouse
The building was erected on the club site in 1965 and is surrounded by a big area of hard standing for yachts. As well as a seven-day bar, dining room and offices, there is a big room for major functions and hire by members. Business occasions are allowed, which is not an unusual feature in Australian clubs. There is a 'bottle shop facility', barbecue area and an area for gaming machines has recently been installed! For the juniors there is a separate building across the boat park.

Waterside
A new 300-yacht marina, costing $A4.5 million is being built. There is already a launching ramp, fuel jetty, slipway and crane. A public jetty adjoins the club land.

History
Because the club was burned down twice, in 1922 and 1954, the historical records are few. The Port Phillip Yacht Club was formed in 1903 and the Sandringham Yacht Club in 1911 on the north side of Hampton Pier. In 1932, the clubs amalgamated, taking the present name, but the burgee of Port Phillip. The second fire was very destructive and the membership dropped to 100, but the Olympic Games gave an incentive to reconstruct and a turning point was the arrival of HRH Prince Philip for the games at the club. He was appointed Commodore-in-Chief and has been ever since. From then on the club's numbers rose.

In 1948 the construction of the rock breakwater had begun. By the sixties the marina was in operation, with a further extension by 1977 and in 1981 the junior building was ready. There are twenty berths for short stay visitors.

Classes
Ocean racing and cruiser racing (IMS, IOR and CHS).

Events and regattas
The club is co-organizer of the 5,500-mile Melbourne to Osaka, Japan Race (1987, 1991, 1995 etc). There are races all year round for the above classes. Racing on Port Phillip every weekend of the year. Seven-day bistro from 1000 to 2359hr every day. Many national and other class associations are able to use the club for prize-givings and meetings.

Members
1,400 : Commodore-in-Chief: HRH Prince Philip.

Address
P.O.Box 66, Jetty Road, Sandringham, Victoria 3191, Australia. ✆ 03 598 7444

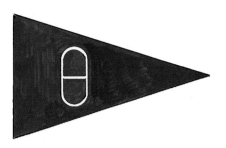

Junior Offshore Group

The name has never really been fully descriptive or satisfactory, but it has stuck and in any case, the club is usually referred to simply as 'JOG'. It organizes offshore races on the south coast of England. There are no concessions to cruising, no inshore racing and no clubhouse. After many years of different courses, it now starts almost every race from Cowes, Isle of Wight, and it is here that secretaries of the group have resided and had their offices since about 1975.

Up to forty boats regularly enter and there are occasionally seventy boats starting in specially sponsored events. The importance of the club stems partly from its single-mindedness on courses in the open waters of the Channel and partly from its historic role in encouraging 'small' yachts on those courses. There are foreign equivalents inspired by its idea. The JOG of Australia has flourished for over thirty years, as have the various Midget Ocean Racing Clubs and Midget Ocean Racing Fleets in a number of parts of the USA. The latter has traditionally had its own rating rule.

Clubhouse and waterside
None

History
In 1949 Patrick Ellam had designed by Kenneth Gibbs, a yacht designer near London, a two-man sliding seat sailing canoe, which was totally watertight and had some stowage. In this he sailed several sea passages up to 100 miles. This was hard going, so next year he consulted Captain John Illingworth, then commodore of the RORC (page 71) about a more 'liveable' design. The distinguished designers Laurent

Giles drew the lines of a 19.7ft (6.0m) wooden clinker sloop with a fin keel and separate rudder on a skeg (unusual for those days). It had a proper little chart table, galley, bunks for two and such safety gear as was the custom at the time.

The yacht was called *Sopranino* and Ellam and one crew took her unofficially on the RORC race to Spain that year. This created a stir, since the minimum RORC size was then 24ft (7.31m)LWL, while *Sopranino* was 17.5ft (5.33m)LWL. The yacht was subsequently (in 1951) sailed across the Atlantic by Ellam and Colin Mudie from England to Barbados. Meanwhile other sailors decided to build sister ships of *Sopranino,* or boats with the same theme, or convert small racers for offshore use.

These people formed, under the presidency of Illingworth, the Junior Offshore Group to give races in open water for boats with a waterline less than 20ft (6.1m). This measurement was soon raised to 24ft (7.31m) which thus catered for all yachts below the size allowed by the RORC. The races varied from around 45 to 180 nautical miles. For the 1954 season Illingworth built an attractive 23.5ft (7.16m) cutter, which won the series in generally hard weather. The crew was three and the JOG did not then allow spinnakers. The group also wrote its own rule of measurement and rating, but after a few years reverted to that of the RORC, which was coming into use for the cruiser races of many clubs.

Despite the enthusiasm of the members, the group did not at first attract many starters. The experience of going offshore in such small boats had limited attraction and during the 50s starts were often in single figures. However the club held on and in the next decade the picture changed as the boats became slightly bigger, most entries being near the top of the range and the boats themselves improving immensely in dryness and speed as the new materials for hull, sails and gear came into use. Boats of good performance began to be used in the short offshore and passage races of other clubs and a 'JOG boat' gradually became less of an unusual creature. Once the Half and Quarter Ton Cups were introduced in the late 60s, standards and international competition increased. The JOG was no longer idiosyncratic. Today the majority of the starters is represented by the modern production high performance yacht. Size limits were gradually widened over the years and now there are none (except that there is a lower limit for the rating figure); starters are usually 'small' yachts, though the sizes of the 50s and 60s have disappeared and there are few entries over, say, 35ft (10.67m). Not many are less than 26ft (7.92m).

Classes
Cruiser-racer and offshore racer complying with current safety and equipment rules. Divided into classes and rated by CHS. No size limits. All races open to non-members.

Events and regattas
About a dozen races per season from April to October, all in the English Channel and varying from 45 to 180 miles. Mostly about 80 miles and about half end in French ports. Seasonal trophies for classes and many permanent cups for individual races. The group has its own start line just to the west of Cowes, based on the private residence of a member. Social events are intentionally very limited and consist only of annual dinner dance with prize-giving .

The reasons for continued support of JOG might be queried in the light of the considerable number of cruiser races available to small yachts and yachts of all sizes in this area. However the ordinary clubs still retain a high inshore element and often more emphasis on socializing than sailing; nor do they frequently provided overnight events, which JOG entrants enjoy. The RORC provides such races, but they are longer, more expensive to enter and, in comparison with JOG, more prone to regulations and paperwork.

Members
400 : There are no flag officers, but a president, captain and vice captain.

Address
Secretary, 43 Parklands Avenue, Cowes, Isle of Wight, PO31 7NH, England.
✆ 0983 280279

The Captain Cook trophy presented to JOG in England by the JOG of Australia.

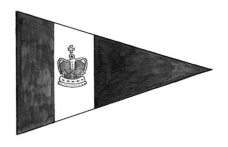

Royal Torbay Yacht Club

Here is a typical English yacht club in a south coast town and holiday resort of 60,000 population. The town is Torquay and Torbay refers to the bay, fully protected from the prevailing south-west wind in which it is situated. The bay is ideal for closed course racing for dinghies and day keel-boats and every year several national championships are held, usually run by the club. In 1948, Torbay was used for the yachting Olympic Games. This coast is sometimes known as 'the English Riviera' owing to the mild climate and palm trees grow along the shore.

Clubhouse
The Victorian clubhouse stands on a road which passes the harbour and though not directly on the water is only a few yards from slipways and a marina, which are within Torquay harbour. Major conversions were made in 1960, so there is a large club room, bar, dining room, snooker room and bridge room. There are men's and women's changing rooms, showers and some lockers for members. The bar is open for 2½ hours each lunchtime and for 5½ hours each evening; in the English manner extensions are available for special occasions. The dining room is open for lunch each day and on Wednesday evening for supper.

Waterside
There is a deep water quay within sight of the club and two concrete launching slips. Short stay is available on pontoon berths and the marina within Torquay harbour has 500 berths.

History
From 1813, regattas in Torbay were organized by the Torquay Royal Regatta Committee, although in 1811 there is a record of a sailing race for ' *boats of not more than 25 feet and to carry not more than 60 yards of canvas*'. The Torquay Yacht Club was formed in 1875 at a meeting in the Queen's Hotel and used the latter for its meetings for some years. A blue ensign, defaced with the club's badge, was immediately granted, together with the title 'royal', which seems strange today and does something to explain the variety of ensigns carried by British yacht clubs.

Ten years later the club amalgamated with the Torbay and South Devon Club (not a club for sailing) and moved into its building of 1825 origin which still stands today. The name of the club became the Royal Torbay Yacht Club.

In the 20s and 30s the club was on the established big yacht circuit around the coast, including the King's *Britannia*; around this time the national championships began, though national classes, as understood today, were a rarity. The International 14 foot class, sailed its big regatta in Torbay, which included (and still does) the Prince of Wales Cup for the class. In 1939, the newly created National 12 foot class held its nationals there.

After the war, the Torquay Corinthian Yacht Club, nearby and with a useful starting platform, ran a share of the racing in Torbay and this site began to be used by both clubs for race starts and finishes. In 1961 both clubs amalgamated and kept the Royal Torbay name. In 1972, there was presented the Torbay Admiral's Cup for cruiser racing in the annual regatta and has since become

The clubhouse (with flagstaff) overlooking Torquay harbour.

well established with many visitors each year. In 1974, the One Ton Cup with a wide international entry was based at the club.

Classes
International Dragon; International Cadet; Dinghy handicap (Portsmouth Yardstick); cruiser-racers (Channel Handicap System and Portsmouth Yardstick).

Events and regattas
Regular racing from April until October on Saturday afternoons and Wednesday evenings. Winter racing October to January for any class with at least five yachts. Torbay Royal Regatta including Torbay Admiral's Cup in about third week of August every year; boats therefore arrive from the Solent after Cowes Week (and in Fastnet years from Plymouth). Most years see the running of three or four national championships (in 1993 these were, for instance, CHS Europeans, Squib, Laser, Cadet). Club yachts take part in nearby Brixham and Dartmouth regattas after the Torbay one. These travel along the coast in the old tradition. RORC races sometimes round marks in Torbay, or finish there. There is a cruising programme of rallies. Annual summer ball, annual dinner, class dinners.

Members
640.

Address
Beacon Hill, Torquay, Devonshire, TQ1 2BQ, England.
℡ 0803 292006

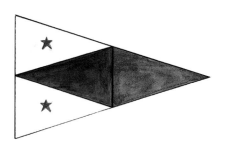

St Francis Yacht Club

San Francisco Bay is one of those sizeable areas of relatively protected water, near large centres of population, where the summer is hot and the result is another major United States yachting area. The extent of the Bay, which is really a salt water lake connected to the Pacific Ocean under the Golden Gate Bridge, is more than thirty-five miles with many small harbours, inlets and marinas, comprising 400 square nautical miles. The area is well known for strong breezes, as the westerly wind pulls in from the ocean. The sailing in the area is a mixture of races and cruising in the Bay and sailing out into the open sea. Fog is quite frequent on the open coast.

Clubhouse
The present clubhouse was completed in 1978, being partly new and partly refurbished portions of the previous building (see below). It is right on the San Francisco city waterfront at the north end and not far inside the Golden Gate Bridge. In 1988, a major extension was made of a starting line room which entailed placement of 90 feet (27.4m) piling on the steep shoreside. The tremendous view from the public rooms is over a large part of the Bay including the entrance under the Golden Gate; also the island of Alcatraz (which is no longer a prison). There is lunch and dinner in the restaurant every day of the year except on Mondays. The latitude is 37° 48' North.

Waterside
There is berthing for short stay and two hoists of 700 feet (213m). Nearby is the permanent berthing of the San Francisco Municipal Marina. Racing courses for large yachts are visible from the club.

History
The first general meeting of members of the newly founded St Francis Yacht Club was held in the Borgia room of the St Francis hotel on the 4th August 1927, the first foundation pile having been driven in for the clubhouse one month earlier. The formal opening dinner for the new building was on the 14th December 1928. A land lease was obtained from the State of California and after negotiations over the years, the building and facilities are now all owned by the club and the land is on long-lease from the City of San Francisco. Both city and club are named after the founders of the original Spanish settlement by the mission of St Francis of Assisi. Thus one of the most affluent clubs is named after a man who founded an order based on poverty.

The economic depression of the 1930s followed soon after the foundation and the club history simply says *they were difficult times, but the doors were kept open*. Recovery was hardly under way when World War II arrived and the club provided a number of volunteer skippers with their yachts, crews and members for hazardous anti-submarine coastal patrols.

Post war prosperity then brought major expansion and a second floor (first storey) was added to the club and a cruising station acquired at Tinsley Island. This gave rise to the Tinsley Island Stag Cruise, a cruise in company followed by a mixture of entertainment and sailing lectures on the island. In 1971 the international ocean racing controlling body met at the St Francis YC and the Tinsley Island Cruise was used for wide discussions and for people from many countries. Since then other cruises, such as for couples and for families have been added.

St Francis Yacht Club, on the marina.

In late December 1976, the clubhouse was mostly destroyed by fire with at least two fatalities. In true American fashion, temporary facilities were established the next day and soon after in close-by sail lofts. When the replacement clubhouse was opened in June 1978, there was not only a dinner, but a week of parties to test out the facilities!

On 14th October 1989 came the San Francisco earthquake (the previous serious one was in 1906) and the only piece remaining of the 1928 building became unsafe. This part, the chart room and offices, was replaced and opened on 23rd January 1991.

Over the years members have helped defend the *America*'s Cup, won the Transpac Race, won the SORC (Florida) and since 1969 won the 6-metre world championship twice with club syndicates.

In nearby waters there are many organizations and the Yacht Racing Association of San Francisco Bay shows forty-nine member sailing and yacht clubs. Among members distinguished in the racing scene are Paul Cayard, Dennis Conner and Bill Koch.

Classes

Many are sailed. Cruiser-racer, offshore racer (IMS, PHRF) and J 24, 29, 30, 105, Express 27 and 37, Olson 30, Newport 30, Santa Cruz 50, Santa Cruz 70, Santa 35, Folkboat. Keelboats: International OD, Knarr, Bird, Beat. Dinghies: International 14, International 505, Laser, Snipe.

Events and regattas

Annual regattas include the Big Boat series (Maxis and large offshore racers around closed courses), Masters Regatta, Aldo Alessio, Woodies Invitational. One or two major championships each year such as Volvo Internationals, Rolex Swan Regatta. The International Star class worlds have been held twice at the St FYC. Social events include Tinsley Island cruises, as above, and cruising events.

Members

2,500.

Address

On the Marina, San Francisco, California 94123, USA.
✆ 0101 415 563 6363

Royal Akarana Yacht Club

One of the world's finest sailing areas is the Hauraki Gulf in the north east of New Zealand. Enclosed on three sides in its southern part, it runs sixty miles north to south in relatively protected waters. Preserved as a national 'maritime park', the waters are immediately accessible to Auckland, by far the largest city in the country. The numerous islands, with their inlets and bays, result in a cruising paradise and the elevation of boating and sailing to a major sport not found elsewhere. There is a high proportion of fresh winds, but the latitude is only 36°south.

Clubhouse
Since 1952, the clubhouse has been at Okahu Bay, four miles east of the centre of Auckland. There has been progressive expansion of facilities for the active membership including club rooms, offices and dinghy launching. The Neptune Lounge and adjoining kitchen can be used for private functions.

Waterside
Auckland regional council has a municipal marina close by the club; both this and the club frontage are protected by a wave break fence. The immediate waters south and west of Rangitoto (within about four miles of the club) have many buoys used for racing marks. Further afield are the waters of the Gulf, as described above, used for cruising and racing.

History
An Auckland regatta was first held in 1840 and in subsequent years for locally designed and built craft, especially the Mullet class, which still exists. The Auckland Yacht Club was founded in 1871 and from 1902 has been known as the Royal New Zealand Yacht Squadron. The North Shore Sailing Club started in 1894 and became the Akarana Yacht Club in 1927, then Royal Akarana in 1937. At that time it was situated in Mechanics Bay in Auckland. The move to Okahu took place when Mechanics came to be reclaimed.

In 1901, the ladies of the club first raced; in 1903, there was a power boat race; in 1931 was held the first trans-Tasman (to Sydney, Australia) ocean race. The first Auckland to Suva Race was in 1956 with 13 starters; in 1977 there was a record 110 yachts, though entries have since dropped to about half of that. Since 1957, the club has presented a Blue Water Medal for any meritorious ocean voyage, racing or cruising. The Royal Akarana has raised teams for the Southern Cross Cup seven times. This series based on Sydney for national and state three boat teams has been won four times by such new Zealand teams. During the period of the International Offshore Rule (1970 to about 1993), club members won the One and Half Ton Cups three times each and the Three Quarter Ton Cup twice.

In general it should be noted that the yacht racing successes of New Zealand sailors in recent years have far outstripped those expected for the size of country and its population.

Classes
Cruiser-racer, offshore racer: using IMS, IOR, PHRF (New Zealand Yachting Federation Performance Handicap Racing Fleet).
Farr 727. International Flying Fifteen.

Events and regattas

Auckland to Suva Race, 1,100 miles, biennial; open national keel-boat championship; women's national keel-boat championship; Farr 727 nationals; Brookes & Gatehouse Gold Cup Inshore series; spring Olympic regatta; Flying Fifteen summer series; summer cruising series; winter series for fully crewed and two-handed.

Members

760 : There is a uniform dress laid down for use.

Address

Tamaki Drive, Okahu Bay, Auckland, New Zealand.
℃ 010 64 9 524 9945

Typical waters around Auckland.

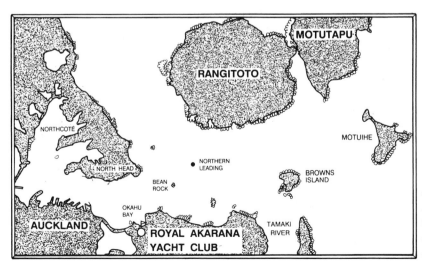

Approaches to Auckland: islands, anchorages, race marks, as well as sun and wind are plentiful.

Upper Thames Sailing Club

Forty miles west of the centre of London, in the prosperous Thames Valley, there is a long established club whose members race intensely on a narrow, but delightful stretch of England's longest river. This fresh water sailing is undertaken by the most modern centreboard dinghies, but there is also an historic class of racing boat dating from the old rating rules of the last century: the 'A' Rater .

Clubhouse
Built in 1970, the clubhouse at the riverside village of Bourne End is the centre-piece of club activities, in effect marking the reach of the river where the races are held. It has a spacious dining room, bar, committee rooms and boat and sail stores. It stands on the site of an earlier club building constructed in 1890 and which was at its last gasp in 1969. It had something of the look of a cricket pavilion, but served the members well. Before even that, two hundred yard downstream was an earlier and smaller clubhouse built about 1885, which turned out to be insufficient. The present club has a caretaker and wife who live in a flat on the premises and as a result provide excellent service.

Waterside
Extensive river bank with slipways and pontoons. The unhurried Thames flows past for ever.

History
A number of members of society living mainly in the town of Maidenhead, met in October 1884 and formed the club in the name which it still retains. There were soon 50 members and then by 1893, there were 120. The first commodore was Lt General Sir Roger Palmer Bt, who owned properties in Dublin, Wrexham and Maidenhead and had been MP for Co. Mayo, Ireland. He had taken part in the famous charge of the Light Brigade in the Crimean War. A number of other distinguished flag officers played a big part in establishing the club; often they owned yachts on the coast and took part in the deliberations of the Yacht Racing Association (YRA) and other bodies.

The YRA though was not very interested in small boat sailing and the club with others formed a 'Sailing Boat Association' in 1888 to look after the non-tidal Thames. Bourne End Week Regatta started almost at once. At one stage it was almost equivalent to Henley and Ascot and was timed to occur between them. In 1893 HRH the Duke of Connaught, third son of Queen Victoria, became president of the club.

Today in the 1990s, the club still gives races for 'Thames Raters'. These are of major historic significance, for they represent the struggles in the 1890s to find an acceptable rating rule. The raters were built to a simple formula of sail area and waterline length and came out at ·75, ·5 (which was a 'half rater') and other chosen figures.The larger boats were 'A raters'.

More than one hundred raters were built and sailed between 1886 and 1906, but only a score or so after that, when centreboard dinghies (the first type to arrive was known as a 'gig') came on the scene. The A raters stayed at Bourne End, but the B raters went elsewhere. One B rater which did stay at the club until 1939 is now in the British National Maritime Museum. In the 1930s,

International 14s and National 12s were given racing. In 1934, the club turned down a proposal to install electric light in the clubhouse. In 1947, the idea of winter racing was discussed. Over the years, the social pattern in England had changed immensely: the landed gentry were no longer essential as flag officers. Instead hard working middle class men and women (though ladies were not allowed to serve on any committee or as flag officers until 1954) took over the leadership of sailing clubs. Harry Scott Freeman was a leading light from the twenties. He was commodore from 1929 until his death in 1967. There was no lack of numerous shrewd and active colleagues in a place like Bourne End and its surrounding area.

In 1980 a glass fibre rater was built and then four more. These were to the same lines as an existing boat built in 1898 to the then rating rule.

Classes
'A' Rater , International 14, National Firefly, National Merlin Rocket, Wayfarer, OK, dinghy handicap (Portsmouth Yardstick).

Events and regattas
Bourne End Week, held annually in May or early June, is the major fixture. The Queen's Cup, presented by Queen Victoria in 1893 is the major trophy. In 1950, a cocktail party was proposed to be held during the week and was opposed by many of the older members who thought it very radical. They were informed that it was not unusual at other clubs, where members had sailed. Today there is a social programme twelve months of the year, including beginning and end of season parties, class evening and mid-summer ball. There are weekend races for all classes and Wednesday evenings with club supper, between May and August. Winter racing goes on until 26th December and racing restarts in March. The Connaught Cup (see the first president above) is an annual handicap prize for all classes over a distance of not less than nine miles.

The raters only race during Bourne End Week, as they are owned by members of the Thames Rater Owners Association and are mostly based at Surbiton, lower downstream. The last wooden rater was built in 1922. There are now eighteen in existence (the five fibre glass ones and the remainder wood).

Members
366

Address
Bourne End, Buckinghamshire, England.
℡ 0753 642041

The clubhouse of the Upper Thames SC on the bank of the river at Bourne End.

Cruising Association

There are clubs which limit membership and keep people out and there are clubs which recruit as many as they can. The CA is one of the latter. Though it goes by the name of 'Association', it is in every sense a yacht club, having personal members, mainly yacht owning, a burgee and privileged ensign and a clubhouse. It is one of that select band of clubs which exist for cruising men and women only (it can be seen in this work that just because the word 'cruising' is in the title it does not mean an organization is 'pure'). The Cruising Association has always been London based, its members mainly live in England, but their voyages extend all over the world.

Clubhouse

Since 1974 the CA has been at Ivory House, St Katharine Dock, London. This group of basins right by Tower Bridge and the Tower of London had been restored and revived within a major plan to rehabilitate the many miles of London docks dating from the 18th and 19th centuries. St Katharine became a yacht marina, where for rather high daily fees, yachts could be almost at the heart of London and a few minutes away from all its attractions. There is no really direct link between the CA and marina, but the building proved suitable and with immensely more atmosphere than the previous clubhouse. The space on the first floor consists of a very big club room lined with bookshelves (for the CA library see below), a bar in one corner and several small rooms off for chart room, offices and a writing room.

The club was due to vacate St Katharine Dock in 1994 and move to another marina on the London River a mile and a half to the east, called Limehouse Basin. There is planned a purpose built clubhouse, with three floors holding all the facilities that have been deemed necessary over the years.

Waterside

Limehouse Basin has been turned into a modern yacht marina. It is necessary to lock in from the River Thames. It must be realised that most members will never take their yachts there; they are based all round the British coast and overseas and make use of the purposes of membership.

History

Although the Royal Cruising Club had been formed in the 19th century (page 83), it had a strictly limited and selective membership and still has today. In 1908, thirty cruising sailors met in London and one year later held the first general meeting which confirmed the committee and an office which produced a register of local boatmen, local representatives and a year book with various information. There followed arrangements for rallies, the establishment of cruising awards in various categories and the beginning of a number of harbour charts.

By 1914 the CA had over 500 members, an annual subscription of one guinea and offices at Denison House, Victoria Street.

After World War I there came to run the CA one of those persons unknown today, a gentleman who took no salary and was full time honorary secretary. He was a cruising man, H.J.Hanson OBE. For forty years he ran the CA himself, kept the subscription down to two guineas and built up an immense and scholarly library, not merely of yachting books. Hanson sailed all round the coasts of Britain, Ireland and the near continent and produced a handbook, which was a unique yachtsman's pilotage guide. In 1930 a new block was opened beside Baker Street underground railway station and the CA moved into a spacious basement area. For forty-two years it was based there, despite the noise of electric trains and the rather austere rooms. By 1939 facilities consisted of a year book with the names of representatives and boatmen around Britain and abroad, the handbook of pilotage, harbour charts, the expanding library, a crewing list, but virtually no social programme except for the elegant annual dinner. The figure of H.J.Hanson brooded over the CA, running it with application, but in his own way. The membership remained at 500, for it was a daunting visit for a new member to the CA rooms with the ever present hon. secretary!

In 1956 Hanson had a serious accident and senior members who entered the club to run it found it extremely difficult to work as, roughly speaking, there were piles of paper and much of the matters in hand merely in Hanson's head. For some years it was a hand to mouth existence with a new secretariat, but the old man, now president, arguing against change. In 1956, Hanson died at the age of 81. Things quickly began to change with increased subscriptions, local rallies, lectures and parties in the CA rooms and the installation of a bar. By 1960 membership had risen to 1,000; in 1970 it was 2,000.

Classes
There are no racing or cruising classes. Members own an immense range of different yachts, mainly sail, but also power.

Events and regattas
The CA has eleven 'sections' all around the British coast and they hold their own meetings, lectures, rallies and events. These are often held at or in local yacht clubs. There are also occasional rallies abroad, for instance in the Mediterranean. The crewing service is a major facility with a continuous filing system, but also arranged evenings for skipper/crew meetings. At major boat shows the CA has a prominent desk, for recruitment and information. The result is a size of membership much larger than was ever imagined in the first sixty years of existence; this means the CA can offer major services to members and there is a permanent staff of about six, as well as numerous honorary appointments.

The availability of books and charts is outstanding. The chart room has classified charts, sailing directions and files of members' voyage tips from all over the world. The library has been reduced, by leasing valuable, historic, but inappropriate books to Cambridge University. This improves their security, brings funds to the club for more applicable publications and releases space. There are about ten trophies awarded annually for outstanding cruises or cruising logs.

Publications: The year book has been published every year since 1908, a journal is published for members about twice per year, the handbook (pilotage) is revised from time to time, (seven editions since inception), corrections are issued annually, deck log to practical requirements.

Members
5,000 : No flag officers. President, three vice presidents, chairman and vice chairman of council.

Address
CA House, 1 Northey Street, Limehouse Basin, London E14 8BT, England
✆ 071 537 2828

Ivory House on St Katherine Dock, London, vacated in 1994.

Purpose-built construction for the Cruising Association in London (seen here in 1993).

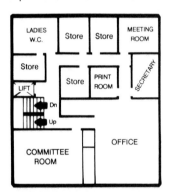

FIRST FLOOR

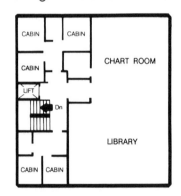

SECOND FLOOR

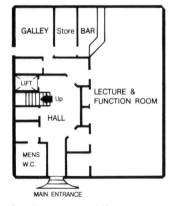

GROUND FLOOR

Plans of the purpose-built, huge-membership Cruising Association clubhouse.

Appendix I

Starcross regatta report in *Exeter Flying Post* 15th September 1775 on the
FÊTE MARINE of 14th August 1775 by the Starcross Club, Devon.

On Monday last the Gentlemen of the Starcross society gave an
Entertainment to their friends at that Place, under the Denomination of a
Fête Marine. - At eight o'Clock in the morning the Exmouth yacht,
accompanied by a Band of Music, came from thence, with several of the
Members of the Society, and having saluted the King's Cutter, and the
Village of Starcross, anchored opposite the Octagon Building in Lord
Courtenay's park, and join'd his Lordship's Yacht, and several more of the
Members'. - As soon as the Tide serv'd they were joined by the Bee Yacht,
and several other Vessels and Boats from Topsham, Lympston, and that
Neighbourhood, about twenty in Number, and full of Company; and having
saluted the Castle, the Cutter, and the Vessels at Starcross, and receiving
proper Returns, they all proceeded to sea, sailed as far as Teignmouth, and
returned back to Starcross at about 4 o'Clock, the Weather being very fine,
and the Wind quite in their Favour: After which several Boats row'd from
the Octagon to the Watch House, and back to the steps at Starcross, for a
prize of ten Guineas given by the society. The platform at the Quay, before
the Courtenay Arms, was rail'd in for the purpose, and laid out in several
Walks, on which a Number of Trees were planted for the Occasion, and
Arches thrown across, on which were several thousand Lamps, which made
a beautiful Appearance. At six the Ladies and Gentlemen, invited to partake
of the Evening Entertainment, came, as soon as it was dark, very curious
Fire-works and Illuminations were displayed, close by the Water-side, which
afforded great Entertainment, as the Evening was remarkably fine, and
then high Water. It was seen at a great Distance, and appeared particularly
well from the opposite shore. At 9 the Ball was open'd, and a handsome cold
supper provided at twelve o'Clock. The Whole was conducted with great
Regularity, and the company departed about 3, well pleased with the
Entertainment they had received; and the whole country seemed to
contribute every Thing in their power to make it brilliant and agreeable.
Notwithstanding the amazing concourse of people, and the Number of
Boats, we have not heard of a single Accident happening. The Fire-works
were mostly prepared and conducted by Sig. Paulo Colpi, and did him great
credit.

On Wednesday the 26th ult. was given at Starcross, (by the Members of
the Starcross Club) a Regatta, supposed to have been the completest ever
given in this county. In the morning Lord Courtenay's yachts, in which were
a number of the Nobility and Gentry, sailed over the bar, with a band of
music &c. accompanied by an incredible number of yachts, cutters, pleasure
boats, &c a general salute of cannon taking place immediately as they got
under way. They returned about four in the afternoon, and were again
saluted by the cannon from the shore, which was lined by an amazing
concourse of people, and every boat and vessel in the harbour was filled. The
compliment was returned from the yachts, and the day proving exceedingly
fine, added greatly to the pleasure and appearance. About eight boats
started for the three prizes, and rowed to the Whale-house on the Warren,
and back again. The prizes were all won by boats belonging to Exmouth.

At eight o'clock the ball commenced, which consisted of near 200 of the
neighbouring Nobility and Gentry. A ball-room was erected for the purpose

at the sole expense, and under the immediate direction of Lord Courtenay, which was beautifully ornamented with artificial flowers, &c. baskets of flowers hung round the room, from whence branch'd large roses which held the candles; the whole forming a magnificent room. The Ladies dresses were very elegant, and such an assemblage of beauty is seldom seen.

The Members did every thing in their power to make all agreeable to their numerous friends. The outside of the ball-room was illuminated with coloured lamps, and opposite stood three beautiful transparent paintings, the one representing Neptune drawn in his car by sea-horses, and on the one side a beautiful boy riding on a sea-horse, on the other side a boy riding a dolphin. At eleven o'clock were displayed very elegant fire-works, which lasted 'till twelve, at which time the company retired to a most excellent supper. The tables were covered with every Variety the season could produce. The dancing continued 'till near four in the morning, when the company retired highly pleased with their entertainment, much to the credit of Mr. Harrison, Lord Courtenay's Cook, who had the direction of the whole entertainment.

It was supposed that there were near 10,000 spectators attended, and a vast number continued in boats, &c on the water the whole night - In short every thing seemed to conspire to render the scene delightful.

Appendix II

Resolutions to form the Yacht Club 1815
At the Thatched House Tavern, St James's Street, London;
1st June 1815, the Rt Hon Lord Grantham presiding,

'First, that the club be called the Yacht Club.'
'Second, that the following persons are the original members of the club:-

Ashbrook, Visct.
Aylmer, Chas.Esqr.
Baring, William. Esqr.
Belmore, the Earl of.
Berkeley, Capt. Frederick.
Blackford, B. P. Esqr.
Buckingham, the Marquess of.
Cawdor, the Rt. Hon. Lord.
Challen, S. Esqr.
Craven, the Earl of.
Curtis, Sir Wm. Bart.
Deerhurst, Visct.
Fazackerly, F.N. Esqr.
Fitzharris, Viscount.
Fitzgerald, John Esqr.
Grantham, the Rt. Hon. Lord.
Grant, Charles Esqr.
Hare, the Hon. William.
Herbert, Henry, A. Esqr.
Hippesley, Sir J. Cox, Bart.

Kirkwall, Visct.
Lewin, Thos. Esqr.
Lindegren, John Esqr.
Lloyd, of Marle, Esqr.
North, the Revd. Chas. A.
Nugent, the Rt. Hon. Chas. A.
Pelham, the Hon. Chas. A.
Ponsonby, the Rt. Hon. Lord.
Puleston, Sir Richard, Bart.
Scott, Harry Esqr.
Shedden, Colonel.
Smith, Thos. Assheton, Junr. Esqr.
Thomas, Sir Geo. Bart.
Thomond, the Marquess of.
Uxbridge, the Earl of.
Wardle, Bayles Esqr.
Webster, Sir Godfrey, Bart.
Weld, Joseph Esqr.
Weld, James Esqr.
Whatley, Colonel.
Williams, Owen Esqr.

and that hereafter the qualification to entitle a gentleman to become a member
be the ownership of a vessel not under ten tons.
'Third, that no vessel under ten tons although belonging to a member shall be
entitled to a number on the list'.
'Fourth, that no person be hereafter admitted as a member without being
balloted for at a general meeting consisting of not less than ten members, the
candidates to be proposed and seconded by two members of the club, two
blackballs to exclude.'

Appendix III

The formation of the New York Yacht Club

On board of the *Gimcrack* off the Battery, July 30th,1844, 5p.m.

According to the previous notice the following gentlemen.assembled for the purpose of organizing a Yacht Club - viz: John C. Stevens, Hamilton Wilkes, William Edgar, John C. Jay, George L. Schuyler, Louis A. Depau, George B. Rollins, James M.Waterbury, James Rogers.

On motion, it was resolved to form a Yacht Club - On motion - it was resolved, that the title of the Club be 'the New York Yacht Club' - On motion, it was resolved that the gentlemen present be the original members of the Club - On motion it was resolved that John C. Stevens be the Commodore of the Club - On motion it was resolved that a Committee of five be appointed by the Commodore to report rules and regulations for the Government of the Club - The following gentlemen were appointed, viz: John C. Stevens, George L. Schulyer, John C. Jay, Hamilton Wilkes, Captn. Rogers.

On motion it was resolved that the Club make a cruise to Newport Rhode Island, under command of the Commodore -

The following Yachts were represented at this meeting, viz: *Gimcrack* - John C. Stevens, *Spray* - Hamilton Wilkes, *Cygnet* - William Edgar, *La Coquille* - John C. Jay, *Dream* - George L. Schuyler, *Mist* - Louis A. Depau, *Minna* - Jas. M. Waterbury, *Petrel* - George B. Rollins, *Ida* - Captn. Rogers.

After appointing Friday 2nd August at 9AM the time for sailing on the cruise, the Meeting Adjourned....

Appendix IV

Dates of foundation of the earliest yacht clubs. For further references, see under specific clubs, also see page 15 on 'which is the oldest club?'

1720 or before Water Club of the Harbour of Cork
1772 Starcross Club (south-west England)
1775 or before Cumberland Sailing Society (or Fleet)
1815 The Yacht Club, later Royal Yacht Squadron
1823 Thames Yacht Club (later Royal) broke off from Coronation Sailing Society ex-Cumberland Fleet
1824 Royal Northern Yacht Club, Scotland
1828 (about) Starcross Yacht Club ex-Starcross Club
1828 Royal Cork Yacht Club ex-Water Club of Harbour of Cork
1827 Port of Plymouth Regatta Club
1829 Royal Gibraltar Yacht Club
1830 Kungelig Svennska Segel Sall Skapet, Royal Swedish
1831 Royal Irish Yacht Club
1833 Royal Western YC ex-Port of Plymouth Regatta Club
1835 Royal Eastern (Scotland) - defunct
1837 Halifax Yacht Club
1838 Royal Hobart Regatta Association
1838 Société des Régates du Havre
1838 Royal St George Yacht Club (Ireland)
1839 Detroit Boat Club
1840 Royal Southern YC ex-Royal Southampton YC, 1838
1843 Royal Harwich YC ex-Royal Eastern (England)
1844 Royal Victoria Yacht Club (Isle of Wight)
1844 New York Yacht Club
1844 Royal Bermuda Yacht Club
1846 Royal Bombay YC, India
1847 Koninklijke Nederlandsche Zeil-en Roeiveeniging, Royal Netherlands Yacht and Rowing Club
1847 Royal Club de Oostende, Belgium
1847 Royal Yorkshire YC
1849 Southern YC, New Orleans
1851 Royal Club de Belgique
1852 Royal Canadian YC
1853 Royal Yacht Club of Victoria (Australia)
1854 Brooklyn YC

Very many clubs were formed all over the world in the second half of the 19th century. The earliest British and European clubs were made 'royal' almost straight away and given royal patronage. This was for various reasons (discussed elsewhere) including the fact that yacht crews were often reservists for the (sailing) navies in the event of war.

Appendix V

The story of the Imperial Poona Yacht Club
Most humbly extracted from an official decree scribed by the hand of a Sahib.

Origins

As this great Imperial Foundation enters its second half-century, a third or even a fourth generation of Sahibs become members. To them, as also to less enlightened fellaheen, our origins may seem shrouded in mystery no less obscure than that of the Indian Rope Trick. Perhaps we should draw aside the veil.

All through the era of the Raj, many who served, whether in arms or as box-wallahs, have returned to these islands carrying with them the traditions, mores and speech of the great Sub-Continent. The prophet Kipling and many others have shown this.

Inevitably we, during our formative years, lived in this atmosphere. At many social events we would be comprehensively regaled with exotic experiences, notably at certain Hill-Stations such as Poona, and Quetta few Simla. One such lengthy debate, on the Fishing Customs of the Hill Tribes of Brahmaputra, was reported in 1934 by Sir Archibald Hope, 17th Baronet, from a Hunt Ball in his Lowland Fastnesses.

This gem of knowledge fired him and his hearers, notably Charles H. Jonston, Arthur Whitehead and Reginald Bennett in the University of Oxford. They decided that a club devoted to the great Anglo-Indian sub-culture and not confined to the more obvious seats of learning was needed.

Accordingly the club came into existence on 22nd April 1934. Membership was limited to fifteen, who must be members of other authentic clubs and must not be married. A burgee was chosen, to a design that was felt to represent the spirit of the Club. A tie was made, suitable for the morning dress worn by members at the weddings of their former colleagues. Mr Gillie Potter, that dignified ornament of the music-hall stage, was good enough to design a cap badge.

Progress

A series of matches and Tiffins took place during the following years, and the Club's colours were flown frequently in events in Imperial Waters on either side of the Atlantic. The seeds of destruction had, however, been sewn in the Club's constitution. Baccalaureate as a condition inevitably brought about a rapid dwindling of the Club's membership. There came in time a moment when, the Club's quorum being four, only three members remained on the strength. Accordingly, in 1938, the three members and the last renegade dissolved the club.

War followed, though not immediately. On the restoration of peace it was obvious that the Yachting community were missing the high ideals of Poona. Suspension of the bar on matrimony enabled a suitable quorum to be formed in 1946. In 1947 the establishment of the club was increased to 25 members.

On the 19th December, 1946, the Club reversed its earlier policy by according recognition to the Y.R.A. It has since recognised the Yachting Association and now the R.Y.A. The process will continue if required.

At a simple though moving ceremony in London on 26th July, 1951, there was established the first Outpost of the Club in the Western Hemisphere - the Revolting Colonies' Outpost - with its own Charter and Thunder Mug, an elegant trophy for coloured racing.

On the 21st Anniversary of the foundation of the Club, 22nd April, 1955, a Charter was issued to the Repulsive but Non-Revolting Canadian Outpost at Toronto. Bill Gooderham became the first and only Commodore.

Pots

In 1956 His Highness the Maharaja of Cooch Parwani generously presented a fine Imperial Trophy for competition annually among the five Clubs at Cowes, sailing keel-boats. In the first twelve completed matches Poona was victorious seven times; and after three consecutive wins in 1965, 1966 and 1967 in I.O.D.'s, S.C.O.D.'s and Darings, Poona was deemed by the Donor to have won outright. The series continued on his re-presentation of the Cup. In 1980 Poona won again at Bembridge. In 1990 the Cup was transferred to the Seaview Mermaids and a new series began, with a Poona victory.

In 1988 Oont Sahib, Hamish Janson, gallantly won for Poona the Cory Cup, the Solent inter-club championship.

Occasions

In 1965, 1967 and 1969 Poona was privileged to show the Flag in the Maharaja's *Bloodhound*. On the last of these three raids on Deauville there was established the Section Batards Normands, based on the Deauville Yacht Club and named in memory of a local Duke who was a member and cruised across channel the other way in 1066. Inauguration took place on 12th October 1969, after which *Bloodhound* was disposed of. In 1976 a further mission was undertaken, in the Gross Vater's *Bottlecry*; and on this occasion Calvados, Cognac and the Medoc were declared re-united with the Raj.

The fortieth Anniversary of the Club's existence, in 1974, was marked by a Durbar most generously held by Maharaja Sahib on board his magnificent Dhow. The Chaplain and Imam of the Revolting Colonists Outpost made a special pilgrimage to this superb event.

The 45th Anniversary in 1979 was duly observed at the Durbar Room, Osborne House, I.W. amid scenes of More Than Oriental Splendour and with the traditional choral accompaniment. Meanwhile the Backward Races, which had been in abeyance for some years, were vigorously revived.

Jubilee

In 1984 our Half-Century, happily coinciding with the Centenary of the O.U.Y.C., was solemnized at the Fuzzy-Wuzzy Sahib's summer palace in the Northern Ghats of Hampshire. In recognition of his distinguished hospitality he was summarily advanced to the rank of Cornucopia.

Jubilee year was marked by the inauguration of an annual series of contests against that remarkable and even longer-established club, The Seaview Buffs. The Thunder Mug was made the prize.

Simultaneously, at the Royal Hong Kong Yacht Club our newest Outpost, the Middle Kingdom Mandarins, was founded by Charter, and in 1986 the Maharaja Sahib held a full Durbar of Mandarins aboard the Celestial Junk after a review of the Outpost's fleet. From this outpost has since flowed a series of erudite works of Celestial, Oriental and Imperial philosophy.

Our fifty-fifth year, 1989, proved a bumper year. In June we won our match against the Seaview Buffs, in glorious weather. The party celebrated, as ever, Fundis birthday and those of Memsahib McPuke and Irrigation Fellah. In July we were lent *Endeavour* by the generous Elizabeth Meyer, helped by our Riggah who had re-rigged his old ship after 50 years. Beating down past Calshot with the double-clawed jib-topsail set was a stirring experience; and an emergency call from Oont Sahib brought from the RYS. a dramatic replenishment of the rapidly dwindling stores. In October the Club, with Memsahibs and Camp-Followers, dined grandly at Skinner's Hall with McPuke Sahib, the Master. The season was brought to a lively finale on Guy Fawkes Day at the Cradle of the Backward Races; for the Thunder Mug.

In 1990 a further Durbar was held at Osborne House; after a suitable interval Poona won the Maharaja's Cup again.

Privileges

Sahibs have kindly been invited to avail themselves of the privileges of the Outposts in existence at the Seawanhaka Corinthian Yacht Club at Oyster Bay, New York, at the Royal Canadian Yacht Club at Toronto, the Royal Bermuda Yacht Club, the Royal Hong Kong Yacht Club and the Deauville Yacht Club. They have also been invited to the privileges of Honorary Membership of the Royal Fowey Yacht Club, of the House of Commons Yacht Club, as also of the Lake Buchanan Yacht Club in Central Texas.

Index to Yacht Clubs

Index to Classes of Boat

OK 157
Optimist 21, 31, 47, 50, 115, 124, 140, 141,
  143
Osprey 131

Pandora 115
PC 90
Pelican 95, 132
PHRF (Performance Handicap Racing Fleet)
  17, 28, 57, 62, 69, 90, 132, 153, 154
PHS 43
Portsmouth Yardstick 31, 46, 80, 115, 117,
  151, 157
Pram 132
Puppeteer 22 141

R-class 90
RNSA-24 97
RORC rating rule 72
Royal Burnham One-Design 36
Royal Windermere-17 82
Ruffian-23 115, 140

S&S-34 145
S22 95
S80 95
Sabot 90
Sandhopper 31
Scow 36
Seabird 93, 131
Seafly 80
Shark 62

Shield 69, 93
Sigma-33 20, 104, 110
Snipe 21, 118, 153
Soling 29, 93, 122
Solo 29, 80
Sonar 69, 93
Sonata 36, 115
Squib 25, 36, 46, 141, 151
Star 62, 90, 132, 143
Surprise 143

Tasar 47
Topper 31, 47, 76
Tornado 29

United Hospitals Dinghy 37

Victory 53
Viking 95

Wanderer 115
Waverley 76
Wayfarer 117, 157
Wight Scow 129

X-99 115

YAH 124
Yeoman 47
Yngling 43
Yorkshire One-design 25

Index